The Peace Dividend

The Most Controversial Proposal in the History of the World

**(Every Citizen's Right to Proper
Compensation for 24 Years
of Fraudulent Wars and
Military Waste)**

by

John Rachel

Published by
Literary Vagabond Books
Los Angeles • Osaka
literaryvagabond.com

LITERARY VAGABOND

Print Book ISBN #978-1-537-58216-0

Cover Art by Penelope Nantucket

Table of Contents

Part I:

Part II:

Part I

The Most Controversial Proposal in the History of the World

The U.S. has become obsessed with war.

The destructive effects of this reverberate through all facets of society and negatively impact the lives of all American citizens.

Halting the current aggressive pursuit of world conquest and Pax America empire, reversing the self-sabotaging and unnecessary build-up of its military power, muting the war drums and arrogant bullying rhetoric, and ending the counterproductive and morally repugnant indoctrination of the populace with war as the only path to peace and world order, are not merely pleasant ideas. They are urgent and fateful requisites.

With the increasing risk of a nuclear conflict between the U.S. and Russia and/or China, prioritizing peace is a matter of survival for the human race.

Nothing about the madness of war fever which grips powerful players at the highest levels of both government and the military-industrial complex is inevitable or irreversible.

But changing the suicidal priorities our nation is now pursuing will take the best efforts of determined activists and a cogent plan.

This succinct book offers such a plan.

It's not without reason that this idea is called "The Most Controversial Proposal in the History of the World".

This isn't because what you will find on these pages is in the least outrageous, impossible, irrational, silly, contentious, divisive, obnoxious, thuggish, or lacking clarity and coherence.

It's because it demands on a level never seen before something which standing governments abhor: Total responsibility and accountability for their actions and errors.

It's because it puts the judgment of citizens above that of arrogant politicos who apparently now believe the consent of the governed is irrelevant.

It's because it calls out blunders and demands proper redress.

History tells us the only way a transformation of this scope and profundity typically occurs is with a violent revolution, when heads roll and the people take back the power they believe they rightfully deserve.

The plan offered here is revolutionary but intended to avoid such a bloody conflict. It is a proposal, not a call to arms.

As will be incontrovertibly established, the U.S. public has been wronged. It has been egregiously insulted and manipulated. Apologies are not adequate, though a good place to start.

No, proper redress will only be achieved by the perpetrators of this fraud on the American public, fully compensating the victims — *you and I!* — and immediately redirecting the energies and resources of our great nation toward serving the interests of all of its citizens. It will require henceforth using military force as an absolute last resort and purely defensively, moreover applying our abundant creativity, our human and national assets, to building a strong and harmonious America, instead of squandering them on "nation building" and imperial adventurism around the globe.

The Peace Dividend is a form of intervention. Our leaders have become drunk on power, addicted to aggression, mentally unstable miscreants plagued by delusions of world empire, pathologically misguided in the bubble of their insularity and own sense of importance.

The Peace Dividend is the first step toward rehabilitation.

The Peace Dividend will quarantine our current errant leadership so they can inflict no further harm on themselves, and more importantly, on innocent Americans and a world that longs for peace. We are in the vast majority and deserve better.

Finally, it will begin to rehabilitate a hapless citizenry which has been compromised morally and financially by the disease of endless war.

Real peace is possible and necessary — more than ever before.

Let's get started.

How did we get here? Or how we fell in love with perpetual war.

Crumbling of the USSR - 1992

In 1992 the USSR — our military nemesis for over four decades of the Cold War — officially ceased to exist. It dissolved. The "Iron Curtain" disappeared. America was declared the only existing superpower in the world.

It was an optimistic time.

No longer was the world to live under threat of nuclear Armageddon.

No longer did we have to devote so much of our time and energy holding the USSR at bay.

We in America in particular were to be the beneficiaries of this "victory" over Communism and the only nation in our history capable of destroying us.

Since far less of the military spending necessary to maintain our nuclear arsenal and vast offensive and defensive weapons systems was required now that the Soviet threat was gone, there would now be plenty of money to devote to other things — better education, parks, schools, a better life for all Americans.

What we were promised was called the "peace dividend".

It never arrived.

In fact, the record shows the military budget for 16 of the next 24 years *substantially increased.*

There was always something we needed, some new military equipment.

But that's only part of the picture.

During the Clinton years and going right up to the present, it seems there was always a conflict to be resolved, a country to be attacked, a war to be fought. We were told we had to save the world and spread democracy.

So we needed even more military junk, more troops on the ground.

Americans were confused, sometimes frustrated.

But they went along.

They shouldn't have.

Because most of the military junk, and most of the conflicts, interventions, rescue missions, bombing raids, invasions, and wars were completely and totally unnecessary.

You name it.

Bosnia.

Panama.

Afghanistan.

Iraq.

Libya.

7

Ukraine.

Now Syria.

All of this conflict … *completely and totally unnecessary!*

Worst of all, so many countries were destroyed, so many people made refugees, so much chaos and anger and hatred created in the Middle East and parts of Europe, with troubles now allegedly brewing in Asia with China, the world is now *more dangerous* than it was before all this started.

After causing so much carnage and destruction, America is now regarded internationally *not* as a beacon of justice and hope, but as the *greatest threat to peace* on the planet.

Nice work, eh?

And guess what?

You paid for it!

The taxpayers of America paid to make it a more dangerous world.

The taxpayers of America paid to make us hated.

Now, who benefited from all of it?

You're not going to like this …

The same people who always benefit from war and other people's misery: The rich and powerful, the wealthy investors who own Lockheed Martin, Boeing, Northrop Grumman, SAIC, General Dynamics, Honeywell, Raytheon, L-3 Communications, United Technologies, Halliburton, Bechtel, Humana, Academi, Huntington Engalls, the list goes on.

You paid.

They profited.

You got poorer.

They got richer.

Your *hard-earned tax dollars*, paid by *you* in good faith, trusting that our leaders would put all that money to proper use, went right into the bank accounts of the rich and powerful, the folks who *already control* most of the nation's wealth — but, of course, won't be satisfied until they have it all.

War is one of the best investments in the world.

Fire tens of thousands of missiles.

Build more.

Fire billions of rounds of ammunition.

Manufacture more.

Blow up whole countries.

Then hire American companies to rebuild them.

Get the picture?

Our roads and bridges are falling apart while we're spending billions to rebuild roads and bridges in Iraq and Afghanistan.

Our schools are falling apart while we build schools in countries most of us couldn't find on a map a few years ago.

During the last 24 years, instead of a peace dividend, we were subjected to the biggest scam in the history of the world.

American taxpayers were ripped off for more than $4.8 trillion dollars! That's *$4.8 TRILLION, with a 'T'!*

Military Waste

Let's back up just a bit.

The phrase I used was 'military junk'. And for good reason.

The Department of Defense is the most wasteful government institution in human history. Just a few things to try to get your head around ...

The F-35 Joint Strike Fighter has been judged by many knowledgeable military analysts as the largest boondoggle in the history of the world. It is plagued with design flaws and technical problems. So far it has cost nearly $400 billion and total outlays to bring it into full production and implementation are projected to exceed *$1.5 trillion.*

The Department of Defense spent $40 billion between 2001 and 2014 on a missile defense program called Ground-Based Midcourse Defense System. It has been a complete flop.

Another missile defense fiasco called X-Band Radar, a floating sea-based system, wasted $10 billion of taxpayer money. This was a project of the Missile Defense Agency, which still gets funded $8-10 billion annually, despite producing practically nothing of value.

At the end of 2014, Congress allocated funds for programs the Pentagon didn't even want:

- $1.46 billion for fifteen EA-18G Growler electronic warfare planes.
- $1 billion to begin work on an additional *San Antonio*-class amphibious transport dock ship.
- $479 million for four additional F-35 fighter jets (bringing the total number funded to 38).
- $341 million to modernize twelve Apache helicopters and nine Black Hawk helicopters.
- $200 million for an additional Joint High Speed Vessel ship.
- $155 million for twelve additional MQ-9 Reaper drones.
- $154 million for an additional P-8A Poseidon Navy surveillance aircraft.

o $120 million for M1 Abrams tank upgrades.
o $150 million for medium and heavy tactical vehicles.

Believe it or not, that's the small stuff.

That's just military garbage which either we don't need or doesn't work.

The Pentagon even has a slush fund for buying stuff they might or might not need, but who's to know, since it's mad money and procurements aren't held to any official disclosure standards. We're talking $60 billion a year!

The Department of Defense is not only the most wasteful government institution in the history of the world, it is the most disorganized.

By its own admission, the DOD can't account for $8.5 trillion allocated since 1996 for the military.

$8.5 trillion!

That's more than the annual GDP of 193 of the 195 countries in the world. All that money was spent on something. We're not sure what.

You really have to ask …

How important can all this stuff be, if no one seems to know what it is?

Now let's talk about *the wars!*

Afghanistan and Iraq

Just look at this chart.

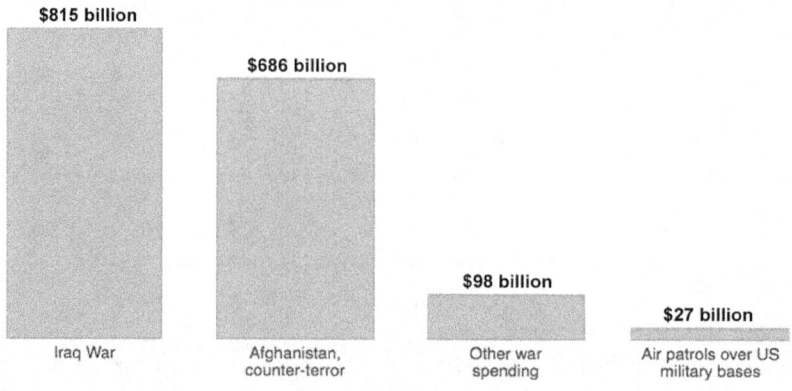

US War Spending Since 9/11
How taxpayer dollars were spent on Iraq, Afghanistan, and other war-related activities

$815 billion — Iraq War
$686 billion — Afghanistan, counter-terror
$98 billion — Other war spending
$27 billion — Air patrols over US military bases

Source: Congressional Research Service

Mind you, we didn't have to fight either the war in Afghanistan or Iraq. There were no weapons of mass destruction in Iraq. We didn't have to go after Osama bin Laden in Afghanistan. The Taliban government offered to hand him over, as long as we wouldn't bomb their country. So we bombed it.

These two wars which so far have cost us $1.5 trillion dollars — and experts have estimated will end up costing us $4 to $5 trillion — were a complete fraud. This is no longer a secret. The lies surrounding both of these fiascos are part of the public record.

Afghanistan, Iraq, and related "counter-terror" spending has cost *you*, the American taxpayer $1.5 trillion dollars — so far. That's almost $5,000 for each man, woman and child living in this country.

Could you use $5,000 right now?

Could you have put it to better use than blowing up countries, killing a lot of people, and having 6,656 of our fine young men and women in uniform come back in body bags?

Could the federal government, which is always crying about how broke it is and how it's unable to balance the budget, have put *some* of that money to good use here at home? Think about this. While our own infrastructure is crumbling, the U.S. government paid out $160 billion — yes, 160 billion of your tax dollars — to rebuild Iraq and Afghanistan. Not $160 billion to repair our schools, build some parks and recreation centers for our children to play in. Not funding for libraries or day care, or nutrition programs. Not funding for senior citizen facilities. No, America spent $160 billion to rebuild two countries we didn't have to destroy in the first place.

At the risk of being repetitious, let's again remind ourselves ...

This is *our* money. These are *your* tax dollars going to waste.

Actually it's worst than just your tax dollars going to waste.

This is *your* tax dollars making a mess of the world and piling up tens of thousands of corpses, often innocent people who were no more to blame than you or your next door neighbor for the trouble in the world.

It would be nice to think that these trillions of dollars did some good, spread democracy and freedom, helped the oppressed, spread hope and love, brought richer more rewarding lives to both ourselves and the countries we have tried to bomb into becoming just like us.

But it never happened.

Again, the politicians painted pretty pictures and made all sorts of joyful promises about what has been going on with all the wars America has started, and the need for the never-ending War on Terror.

Again, the pretty pictures were and still are just that, and have no relation to reality.

Again, the promises made are just more hot air and empty rhetoric.

Many of our soldiers paid with their legs and arms, their eyesight and hearing, their sanity and ability to function, even with their lives.

We paid with money we could have used for ourselves and our loved ones.

We bought ...

Military junk.

Unnecessary wars.

The endless War on Terror.

These add up to the most expensive blunders in the history of the world.

Taxpayer Money Wasted Over 24 Years by the DOD

I recognize the obvious.

There are problems in the world.

There are enemies out there. There are bad people.

Not as many as our military establishment and political leaders would have us believe.

But they're there.

Thus, it is essential that America properly defend itself against possible attack by rogue nations, cells of terrorists, bands of militarized thugs.

A reasonable amount of defense spending is just the proper price of safety and survival, true for any nation, even more so for one occupying a uniquely prominent and powerful position in the world.

What I *don't believe* is that this represents a blank check to purchase anything some wild-eyed daydreamer in the Pentagon decides we must have, a carte blanche to start conflicts anytime someone looks at us cross-eyed, tacit open-ended permission to "project" America's military power as a lever to secure foreign markets and resources, or license to create a constant state of war across several continents just because we can.

This is exhausting both the treasury and the spirit of this country.

People are sick of war.

And now that the lies leading up to our two largest recent wars have become known to the public, it is obvious that both Afghanistan and Iraq were disastrous mistakes.

Taking all of this into consideration, I have arrived at an accounting of what all the waste and misadventures have cost *us*, the good and decent taxpayers of this country, over the past 24 years.

Many hours and a lot of research went into coming up with a total figure, representing the theft and misuse of *our* money.

Mind you, this accounting is actually very conservative.

It's based on the "official public budget" of the Department of Defense.

There are all sorts of defense expenditures and top secret programs that are tucked inside other departmental budgets, or off-budget entirely. This year over $12 billion is hidden in the Department of Energy budget for nuclear weapons. More than $60 billion goes for what's termed the "black budget" of the NSA.

Then you have the billions and billions going to 1,271 government organizations and 1,931 private companies working on counterterrorism programs, homeland security and intelligence, allegedly making us safer. You have to wonder if ISIS, al Qaeda and al Nusra are getting a good laugh out of that. The safer we get, the more terror they inflict on innocent people in Europe, the Middle East, beheadings coming soon to the U.S. of A.

The final insult: While bridges, roads, schools, communities fall apart, and entire cities like Detroit become wastelands here in America, the U.S. government using our tax dollars has spent more rebuilding Afghanistan and Iraq, than it did rebuilding Germany after World War II. Over $100 billion has gone into reconstruction in Afghanistan so far, and $60.45 billion in Iraq.

It just goes on and on, eh?

Here's what my research shows has been wasted:

American Taxpayer Money Wasted Over 24 Years by DOD

EXCESSIVE BASIC D.O.D. SPENDING: 1993 - 2016	$2,721,000,000,000
AFGHANISTAN WAR: 2001 - 2016	686,000,000,000
IRAQ WAR: 2003 - 2015	815,000,000,000
OTHER WARS: 2001 - 2016	98,000,000,000
AIR PATROL PROTECTION U.S. BASES: 2001 - 2015	27,000,000,000
EXCESSIVE N.S.A. BLACK BUDGETING: 2001 - 2016	293,000,000,000
UNNECESSARY D.H.S. SPENDING: 2003 - 2016	186,000,000,000
TOTAL DUE:	**$4,826,000,000,000**

The biggest chunk of this astonishing total — over half — results from factoring in the "peace dividend" the American people were originally promised back in 1992, but never received. While it was reasonable to assume based on all of the rhetoric back then, that the total DOD budget would *come down* — and it actually did for 8 of the 24 years — my calculations were based on holding it steady at exactly the level it was in 1992. Some of the increases from that $380 billion figure were modest, then they started to skyrocket. This year's defense budget is double what it was in 2000, just to give you some perspective on how wild the spending increases have been. As stated before, this is probably on the low end. Still, at bare minimum over the past 24 years, the wars, the insane military build-up, our building over 900 bases in 136 countries, the funding of boondoggles like the F-35, the enormous expansion of the national security complex, much of it housed in or funded by the bloated Department of Homeland Security, conservatively has squandered $4.82 trillion of our tax money.

That's trillion!

I repeat, for those of you who may be in shock, $4.82 TRILLION!

Here's what $4.82 trillion dollars looks like in $100 bills:

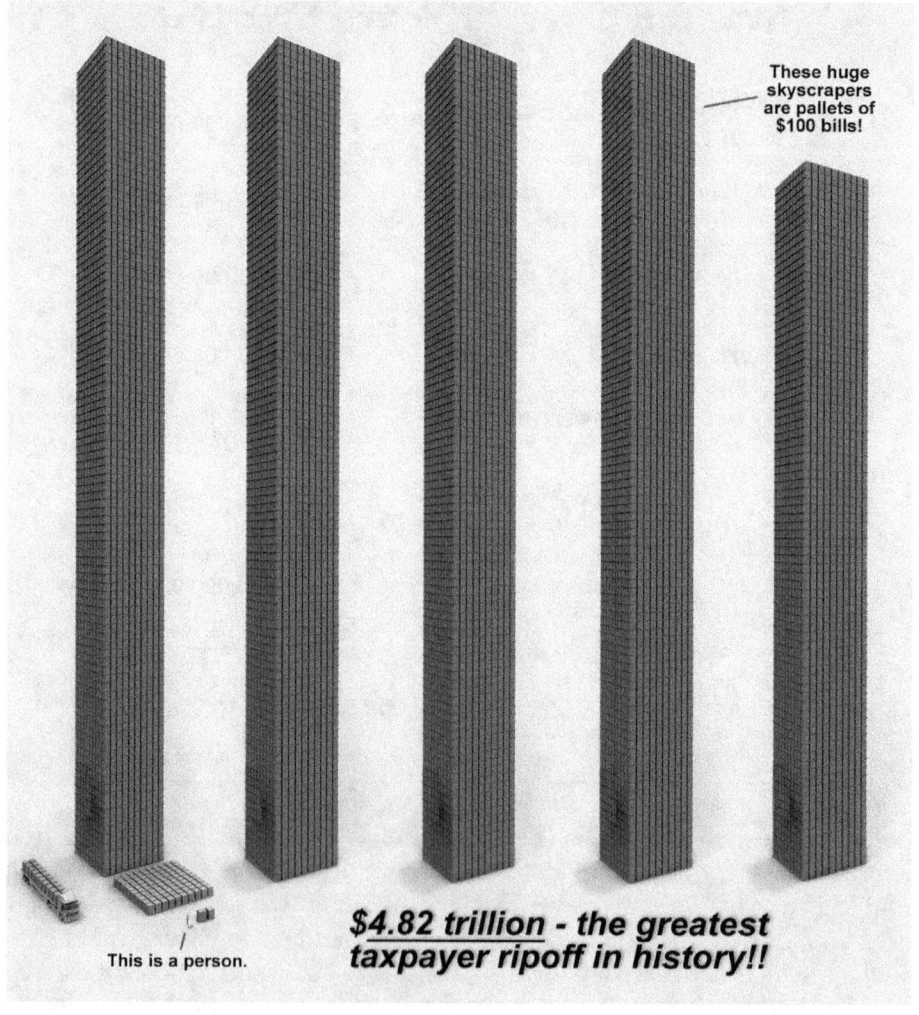

These huge skyscrapers are pallets of $100 bills!

This is a person.

$4.82 trillion - the greatest taxpayer ripoff in history!!

Does this put in perspective why we should judge this the most odious and irresponsible ripoff of tax dollars in human history?

This outrageous total representing the fraud inflicted on the American public is a result of constant war: Two major wars that we were lied into — consequently never should have been fought — that *you* paid for. And the rest represents the war our elected officials have been conducting on the truth. And us personally! The wars on our families, our schools, the war on each of us, the pillaging of our bank accounts, their taking our hard-earned money under false pretenses, then throwing it down the drain. *We demand ...*

No more destructive, wasteful, criminal wars.

But that's not all. *We want our money back!* We want a refund. All of it! All of the money fraudulently taken from Americans for military scams and the horrific wars we were lied into. The bill is immediately due and payable.

We want our *Peace Dividend*.

The Peace Dividend: Recovering Lost Money and Time

Here's the plan.

$4.82 trillion was paid in good faith by American taxpayers.

Nothing of value came of it.

Nothing! It was a total rip-off.

So ...

We're going to get our money back!

The Peace Dividend promised in 1992 *will finally be paid.*

Here's how it works.

Since I've decided against making this complicated, my method is simple, straightforward, equitable, fair and honest. It's basic math.

There are exactly 322,762,018 U.S. citizens as of July 4, 2016.

Divide that into $4.826 trillion and you get $14,952.

I propose this be paid to each and every American citizen, divided up evenly over three consecutive years.

$4,984 paid to each and every one of us each year, three years in a row.

All that is required is that you are a U.S. citizen.

If you are a member of a typical family of four, your family will receive $19,936 each year, three years in a row.

I think this will help out.

Don't you?

Making It Happen!

There is a sure way to make this happen.

First you and at least 50 million other Americans have to believe in it.

Then you need to stand shoulder-to-shoulder with these other citizens.

You need to remain strong and *insist* on just treatment, understanding that having *your* hard-earned money returned to you is well within your rights in a democracy of the people, by the people, and for the people.

Knowing we have your full support, *we* then need to present a demand to every single candidate running for federal office, requiring them to initiate all necessary legislation and related measures to send you your Peace Dividend checks, starting the first congressional session after the next election.

There *are* candidates who will agree to this, guaranteeing you your share of the Peace Dividend refund. We will find them and let you know.

Be forewarned, however.

Most of the incumbents, mainstream politicos, and their puppet pundits will scream bloody murder and throw histrionic tantrums.

It's not their style to offend their rich benefactors.

And you can count on this: The rich and powerful will fight this tooth and nail, with everything they can bring to the battle.

Let's be blunt about it.

They pay you as little as possible on the job, slash your benefits, steal your pension money, cut school programs, refuse whenever they can to pay unemployment compensation and try to screw you out of your social security — both of these are your money as well, not even tax money, but money you have paid into special accounts, the unemployment insurance fund and the social security trust. They bust up your unions, ship your jobs overseas to pay some 13-year-old kid a couple dollars a day to do your work, jack up medical and prescription drug costs while hacking away at Medicare, make education almost unaffordable and loan you money to go to college which will take you ten years to pay back. They seduce you into home loans you can't afford, then repo your house and throw you and your family out in the street.

You think they're going to take kindly to having Uncle Sam pay you back the money the government stole so they could fight wars and see their defense industry stock shoot through the roof?

Moreover, the ultra-wealthy are really going to have a conniption when they realize to pay for the Peace Dividend — full explanation on how it will be funded is in the next section — their taxes are going to go up ... way up!

But why? If they're decent citizens, what right do they have to object?

First off, it's their public duty and responsibility to the country to pay their fair share.

Second, it was the filthy rich who got richer off of that $4.82 trillion. Their ownership of defense companies, their pushing America into wars, selling the DOD on all sorts of wonderful, if unnecessary, military hardware and, and their insisting on military deployments to protect *their* investments all across the globe, *that's* where that money went.

Essentially from your pocket into theirs.

Of course, that's not something the rich and powerful will admit.

They'll carry on about class warfare and communism and socialism and how the sweaty masses are stealing their hard-earned fortunes.

Believe me, it's going to get ugly.

But no matter what *they* say, remember ...

This is <u>our</u> money. This is money we could have used. If we Americans had had the $4.82 trillion, we wouldn't be so far in debt, we wouldn't be struggling, our economy wouldn't be stumbling. We would have put it to good use. We now deserve to have it back, so that belatedly, we <u>can</u> put it to good use. To improve our homes, clothe, feed and educate our kids properly, pay off some of our credit cards.

You paid your taxes in good faith.

You never had a say in how your tax dollars would be used.

You certainly would never have agreed to see the $4.82 trillion wasted the way it's been wasted.

You were told to trust and have faith in the judgment and decisions of those in charge of foreign policy and the nation's defense.

You *did* trust them to do the right thing.

But that turned out to be one *huge* mistake.

The money was not put to good use. It did not increase your safety. It did not improve the quality of life for you and your family. *You* got nothing for forking over your hard-earned dollars.

Just apply some common sense here ...

Say you buy a fruit blender or a hair drier from a store, and when you take it home you find out it doesn't work. What do you do? You return to the store, then either get a replacement or you get your money back.

Unfortunately, there's no way to get a "replacement" for anything the $4.82 trillion was squandered on. Even more tragically, we can't bring back to life the brave men and women whose lives were lost in the senseless wars. We can't turn the clock back.

But what we can do is <u>get our money back</u>.

Let's face the facts. We didn't just get a defective fruit blender or broken hair drier. We got defective wars, defective military equipment, defective leadership. We got a defective economy where only the rich do well and for the rest of us it's broken. Since they wasted our trillions of dollars, now we have broken bridges, broken roads, broken schools, broken communities.

We have broken homes!

We have bankruptcies and foreclosures.

We have unemployment and underemployment.

Enough!

We're going to get back *all* of this money. It's our money. We paid it to our government in taxes. We trusted them. And they abused our good faith. They lied to us.

There's nothing to quibble about here.

There's nothing to negotiate.

We want our money back.

We _demand_ our money back.

Period!

Every single candidate running for office needs to understand.

Then the American public must stand together and stand strong on this.

We have had it with being taken for granted.

We will no longer be an ATM machine for the kind of foolishness we have endured for the past 24 years.

So ... right after those responsible for this theft of our taxpayer money _apologize_ for this crime against good decent people, we expect them to start cutting checks to every U.S. citizen to make amends for this disgraceful abuse of power.

Amen.

A New Direction for America

Yes! This Is For Real

No, the Peace Dividend will not bankrupt the country.

No, it's not bad for the country.

In fact, it's *good* for our the country.

It will give the economy a much needed boost.

It will put money in the pockets of everyday Americans, people who will spend it and get our consumer-based economy moving again.

And yes, *we can afford it.*

There are a number of mechanisms in place, legal and fiscal, which can more than adequately cover this refund of taxpayer money.

What Goes Around Comes Around

Without getting into all of the fine details, here is an outline for precisely how the Peace Dividend can be funded.

1) Peace bonds.
2) Massive tax reform.
3) Financial transaction taxes.
4) Taxing offshore assets and offshored cash.
5) United States Dollars (a peace-based currency for domestic use only).
6) As a last resort, minting large-denomination coins.

This will not produce more irresponsible debt — this combination is not built around frivolous borrowing. In fact, it introduces into the monetary and investing systems which are now at the core of our economy, elements which vastly accelerate growth, invite responsible investment, and share the fruits of the entire enterprise with *all* Americans.

Items #2, #3, and #4 are self-explanatory.

Essentially, the Peace Dividend *drives* a whole array of tax reforms.

For example: boosting the basic income tax over $250,000 to 50%, over $1,000,000 above 60%, on up the income scale. Then, coupling increases in capital gains rates to income tax rates — so the wealthy can't reduce their tax liability the way they do now by transferring their wealth into capital assets — finally, making similar adjustments to taxing corporations.

It also drives reduction and elimination of unnecessary tax breaks and various subsidies.

Perhaps more importantly, it introduces a whole new set of laws which attaches responsibility for taxes to offshored accounts and investments, and market speculation. It drives restructuring the chartering of corporations and introducing regulation *discouraging* exporting facilities and jobs; imposing huge fines and penalties for moving and basing manufacturing and services overseas. This is a source of substantial revenues for the federal government.

To understand item #6, it should be recognized that the U.S. government is well within its constitutional rights to create such coinage. It's in Article 1: The Legislative Branch, Section 8: Powers of Congress:

> The Congress shall have Power To lay and collect Taxes, Duties, Imposts and Excises, to pay the Debts and provide for the common Defence and general Welfare of the United States; but all Duties, Imposts and Excises shall be uniform throughout the United States; To borrow money on the credit of the United States; To regulate Commerce with foreign Nations, and among the several States, and with the Indian Tribes; To coin Money, regulate the Value thereof ...

Since items #1 and #5 will likely contribute the majority of the funding — assuming option #6 is not exercised in whole or in part on an epic scale — more detailed explanation of these might be helpful.

Neither — obviously the issuance of bonds but also the creation of special purpose currency — is unprecedented. However, under the terms of the proposed plan, the implementation of each of these is somewhat unique.

Peace Bonds

Funding war has always been a priority. Funding peace is another matter.

In World War I, the U.S. issued *Liberty Bonds* to raise money for the war. Before World War II, Series E, F and G *U.S. Savings Bonds* were being promoted. Right after the attack on Pearl Harbor, these were sold as *War Bonds*. After the war, the name was switched back.

Many older readers will remember U.S. Savings Bonds being popular when they were kids. They were promoted as birthday and graduation presents and remained in the spotlight right up until five to ten years ago, when people were no longer inclined or able to save money, therefore they stopped buying them.

I can find no record in our history books of anything called *Peace Bonds* in America.

There should be.

If we can raise money for war, we sure as hell can raise money for peace.

For people who actively want to promote peace, some of the money they get as a refund could be invested back into funding the Peace Dividend.

Meaning, those individuals who aren't pressed for immediate cash, thus don't need the entire amount of cash payment for their Peace Dividend refund right away, could opt to receive all or part of it as *Peace Bonds*, an investment in America's future that would accrue interest and be part of national commitment to focus on peace instead of war.

Once the Peace Dividend refunds are covered by whatever combination of tax and monetary devices works, *Peace Bonds* could be sold on the global bond market, inviting other countries to invest in America's peace initiatives. Such efforts could include addressing at an international level poverty and health issues, building Third World infrastructure, and other projects which would reduce aggression and conflict, and promote harmony in the world.

I'm not meaning to sound like a neo-hippie fruitcake here, but *Peace Bonds* should play a much-needed role in shifting the national consciousness and narrative away from war, perhaps even rehabilitating America's image in the international community as a war-obsessed bully. It seems everything in America now is about the military, war, fighting, bombing, droning. The peace movement is all but dead. Just seeing the word 'peace' *occasionally* might be a refreshing change. It might steer people to thinking about peace as a purposeful and relevant pursuit.

Which brings up item #5, the issuance of special domestic use currency.

United States Dollars

To reiterate, special use currency is not unprecedented.

Abraham Lincoln used "greenbacks", a paper currency backed by nothing more than confidence in the government, to finance the Civil War.

A century later, on June 4, 1963, John F. Kennedy signed Executive Order 11110 which set in motion the issuance of silver certificate notes, currency backed by silver reserves being held at that time by the U.S. Treasury. This bypassed the established procedure of borrowing money into circulation from the Federal Reserve. $20 billion of such United States Notes were put in circulation before he was assassinated, many believing it was his introduction of such interest-free debt-free currency which actually may have prompted his murder.

Risk of assassination aside, no reasonable case can be made against using this power. It is guaranteed by the Constitution (see Article 1, Section 8 above). Our current debt-driven system requiring us to borrow from the private banking institution misleadingly named The Federal Reserve to inject money into the economy is absurd and in the long term counter-productive.

While ultimately our goal should be to totally eliminate the Federal Reserve's role in this process, for now we can pick up where Kennedy left off, prudently using what we call *United States Dollars*, to cover a sizeable portion of the Peace Dividend refunds.

United States Dollars would look almost exactly like their Federal Reserve Note counterparts. Same layout, same denominations, same founders-of-the-nation and presidential images.

Where U.S. currency now says ...

FEDERAL RESERVE NOTE

... *United States Dollars* not surprisingly would say ...

UNITED STATES DOLLARS

Where U.S. currency now says ...

IN GOD WE TRUST

... *United States Dollars* would say ...

PROMOTING PEACE

Where in nearly microscopic print U.S. currency now says ...

THIS NOTE IS LEGAL TENDER
FOR ALL DEBTS, PUBLIC AND PRIVATE

... *United States Dollars* would say ...

THIS NOTE IS LEGAL TENDER FOR ALL DOMESTIC
FINANCIAL TRANSACTIONS, PUBLIC AND PRIVATE

Please note: *United States Dollars* would be for <u>domestic use only</u>. This is to prevent them from being shipped overseas or feeding them into the ongoing currency speculation frenzy. Banks would be instructed to block transfer of *United States Dollars* equivalencies to non-domestic banking institutions. For example, if a person deposited $8,000 of *United States Dollars* into a domestic account, transfer of funds to non-domestic banks or use of funds for purchases outside the U.S. could only be made from balances his or her account in excess of $8,000 accruing from Federal Reserve Note deposits.

This restriction is to guarantee that *United States Dollars* go toward promoting America's <u>*domestic economy*</u>, i.e. purchasing goods and services "Made in the USA". This precludes exporting any of this newly generated wealth, which would only exacerbate our already excessive and out-of-control trade deficit.

Private banks would be encouraged to create *United States Dollars* credit cards. If there is institutional resistance to this by private banks, the U.S.

government can fill that need by issuing through its own agencies such credit instruments.

A host of small-business and employee-owned business incentives could be built around *United States Dollars*, for example giving matching federal grants or at least preferential treatment for investing *United States Dollars* in job-creating domestic business start-ups.

All of this points the economy in a hopeful and highly constructive, new direction. The expansion of general usage of *United States Dollars* down the road could gradually dismantle the current Debt Doomsday Machine of the Federal Reserve regime. Imagine Congress arguing over the size of budget *surpluses* instead of budget deficits!

Wouldn't that be refreshing?

You're An American Citizen ... You Deserve Respect

Yes, we can expect desperate cries of outrage to issue from the solemn faces of the plutocracy, both with respect to the Peace Dividend and the methods proposed here for funding it. But the truth is ...

You deserve better.

You deserve respect and fairness.

You don't deserve to be used and abused.

The Peace Dividend is a proper refund for a defective product.

It's your money being returned to you to put to good use, building a better life, stronger communities, a productive and robust economy, an America that works for all of us, not just the rich and powerful.

So ...

Put your future congressman, your future senator, every candidate now running for president, put them *all* on notice.

If they can't get behind rectifying this gross injustice against American taxpayers — against *you* — then you will find someone who will.

Go to our three sister organization sites and join the signature campaign:

http://peacedividend.us
http://50-million-signatures.us
http://we-want-our-money-back.us

For America to be strong, Americans must be strong.

For America to be strong, American families must be strong.

For America to be strong, American families must be solvent.

$14,952 for each American citizen.

A newly married couple will receive $29,904 to get a start in life.

A family of four will receive $59,808 to pay down their credit cards, buy the kids some new clothes, fix up or replace that car that's falling apart.

If the American government can magically come up with trillions of dollars to bail out the banks, or trillions of dollars to fight stupid unnecessary wars, it surely can come up with $14,952 to help each U.S. citizen get his or her life on track.

I've shown how this can work.

You've seen the plan.

Let's do it!

Part II

Fool me once . . .

Demons

Militarization and preparation for war are driven by fear.
Fear is propagated by creating demons.
Let's look at some of our current demons.

Russia Bad America Good

The demonization of Russia among Western journalists has gotten so perverse, if Vladimir Putin were to jump in an active volcano and rescue a family of four Americans, carrying them on his back hobbling along on the melted stumps of his legs to a hospital 50 miles away, the mainstream media in the U.S. would report that Vlad the Impaler in some disconnected attempt to reconstruct the Soviet Empire had personally kidnapped four defenseless U.S. citizens and was holding them in a labor camp in the Siberian tundra.

Nothing good about Russia ever makes the cut these days, only the bad, much of it fabricated by the U.S. government itself. Even indisputable facts of history take a back seat to vilifying everything Russian. With appalling disrespect, Western leaders snubbed Russia by refusing to attend the 70th anniversary celebrations of victory over Germany held in Moscow in 2015. Then at equivalent ceremonies in Europe, scant mention was even made of the Russian campaigns, which resulted in the deaths of over 10 million Russian soldiers. If you actually bother to check the record, you will discover it was not France, England, and the U.S. which defeated Hitler. It was Russia.

I don't say this because I'm a Russia lover or a Putin apologist. This is a matter of historical record. Maybe to the propagandists in the West with their highly focused, patently obtuse agenda, facts don't matter. But to you and I, if we are to have any shot at all at embracing harmony in the world, facts are vital to a greater appreciation of a nation of 170 million people whose government is armed with over 7,000 nuclear warheads.

Here are some more facts. Feel free to check the historical record:

Did you know that Joseph Stalin proposed in 1952 that Germany be reunited as a single neutral country with free elections? The main condition was that Germany not be part of a NATO alliance, which it viewed as a military threat. Russia was under enormous pressure economically after being ravaged by World War II and wanted to reduce the growing tensions between the East and the West.

Of course, by ridiculing and ignoring this proposal it would take another forty years of Cold War hostility and posturing to reunite Germany, then as an loyal ally and military stronghold of the U.S. — though interestingly Germany now is one of Russia's most important European trading partners.

Did you know that prior to the 1963 Cuban missile crisis, Nikita Khrushchev for almost a decade proposed substantial reductions in offensive weapons? That while America was implementing the largest peace time military build-up in history, Russia was in fact reducing its military capability?

Khrushchev finally became convinced, especially after the U.S. placed in nearby Turkey nuclear-tipped Jupiter missiles which could easily reach Russia, that America was bent on attacking the Soviet Union. *This* was the underlying reason for deploying nuclear missiles in Cuba, precipitating one of the most dangerous crises in history. Perhaps not the wisest thing to do, given the level of tensions the U.S. maintained with its constant "better dead than Red" fear mongering, nevertheless the missiles in Cuba were basically the Soviet's attempt to achieve some sort of parity, at least a minimal acceptable level of mutually assured destruction with America.

Did you know that in 1983 the U.S. risked starting World War III with provocative and unnecessary probing of Soviet air defenses? This was purely a strategic and psychological maneuver intended to bolster support Reagan was soliciting from Congress and U.S. allies for his Star Wars missile defense system. Because at this same time the U.S. was deploying nuclear-tipped Pershing II missiles in Europe which only had a 5-minute flight time to key targets in Russia, Soviet leadership understandably viewed Star Wars not as a defensive system but as the means for establishing a first-strike capability. And it suspected the probing of its air space and testing of its defense systems was a prelude to an attack. Speculation about a first-strike nuclear attack on Russia continues to this day.

Did you know that both Reagan and Gorbachev in the end were quite sincere about totally eliminating nuclear weapons by the end of the 20th Century, that their verbal agreement during a summit in Reykjavik, Iceland to work toward eliminating the nuclear arsenals of both Russia and the U.S. was quite authentic? It was not posturing. Moreover, did you know that the whole idea for eliminating the entire nuclear arsenals of both countries was initiated by Soviet Premier Gorbachev in a letter sent to President Reagan January 14, 1986? It was actually *his* idea.

Did you know that Russia only has ten foreign military bases? This is in contrast to what many estimate to be nearly 1000 in at minimum 156 countries by the U.S. A cursory glance at a world map shows that a substantial number of these bases form a ring around Russia. Even the most impartial observer would not view this as a coincidence and would at least appreciate why Putin and company see much of what America does as provocative, if not blatantly confrontational — why some analysts *on both sides* conjecture that America is preparing to launch a "preemptive" nuclear attack on Russia, begging the question what such an attack would preempt other than the continuation of the human species.

Did you know that contrary to headlines which screamed foul in the American media, Russia never invaded Crimea? The simple fact is that there were 16,000 troops already stationed there, as per a standing treaty with the Ukrainian government. When the elected President of the Ukraine, Viktor Yanukovych — certainly corrupt and questionable in his own right — was run out of the country by street thugs, understandably these troops were instructed to protect key physical assets in the region, as well as make sure that the many native Russians who were living there remained safe. There was no firefight, no resistance. After over 4/5th of eligible voters demanded in a internationally-monitored referendum to rejoin Russia, the region which had been part of Russia going back to 1786, returned to Russian authority — hardly an *invasion* by any stretch of the imagination. No troops stormed over the border. No shots were fired.

Did you know that far from being the instigator of the current crisis in the Ukraine, Putin has consistently played peacemaker and attempted to defuse the situation, even as native Russians came under threat from the new government in Kiev, and now are mercilessly being slaughtered in order to ethnically cleanse the Ukraine of all Russian influence? Neo-Nazis now comprise the shock troops rampaging through the eastern regions and assaulting Donetsk and Luhansk, the two strongholds of pro-Russian separatists.

Moreover, contrary to the narrative being pushed by the White House — obviously the work of neocon ideologues still infesting the government in the State Department and think tanks within the beltway — the evidence is quite clear that the entire coup was engineered and directed by the U.S., using agent provocateur NGOs, funded by National Endowment for Democracy. Senator John McCain and Asst. U.S. Secretary of State Victoria Nuland were even on the front lines during the demonstrations. This is, of course, not what you were being told by the American press, which with the White House itself leading the charge continues to pin all of the blame on Russia and Putin.

Now am I making a one-sided case here? Of course not. There have for over six decades, extending right up till the present, gross deceptions and blunders on both sides. I bring up the above examples because the collective memory of the American public seems to be very short. Or more likely, many well-meaning Americans may not even be familiar with these particular facts in the first place. Anything good about the Soviets — and now the Russians — tends to be overwhelmed and replaced by the firmly entrenched and much easier to embrace "black hat" characterization we now hear regurgitated over and over.

What I am saying is there has already been so much misunderstanding, miscalculation, and missed opportunities, that to compound our bleak and tendentious relationship with Russia with more misunderstanding, miscalculation, and missed opportunities, is courting disaster. It's that simple. What's been going on is not working. Time for a new approach.

And I am also saying that America lately bears more than its share of responsibility for the distortions, the slander, the disinformation, which has aggravated hostility toward Russia both by leaders in their official capacities, and now by American citizens, who never seem to run out of foreign peoples to fear, mistrust, even hate.

Let me throw something else into the mix here. This is probably the most important factor whenever we look at Russia and try to gauge her motives and intents.

The Soviet Union lost more than 21,000,000 people in World War II. Most were killed in the Russian homeland itself as a result of the overwhelming German Nazi blitz. Over a half million died in the Battle of Stalingrad alone.

That is why they are fearful of having troops and/or ballistic missiles on their borders — as in the Ukraine or Georgia. They have been gritting their teeth as NATO has edged its way closer and closer to Russia — contrary, by the way, to reassurances given right after the fall of the Berlin wall and the reunification of Germany. America lost 420,000 soldiers during all of World War II, fighting on two fronts, in Europe and the Far East. If we had seen

22,000,000 Americans killed, the blood of the majority spilled right here on our own soil, how would we feel about having troops, nuclear-tipped tactical missiles, and ballistic missile defense radars and interceptors arrayed along the Canadian or Mexican borders? How would we read the intention of any nation insisting on putting these on our borders?

As they say, this is not rocket science.

What might require the intellectual aptitude of a rocket scientist is trying to understand what America's strategic planners have in mind in promoting this agenda. It undermines any possibility of peace between the two great powers and risks thermonuclear war.

Am I a Russia lover?

An America hater?

Neither.

I just think that before we kill a few more million people or destroy the world, we might want to look at both sides of each issue, maybe mentally trade places, try to be fair and reasonable, give our all to try to understand exactly what is going on.

And a big part of understanding issues is knowing history, taking into consideration what has been occurring for decades, sometimes even centuries. To paraphrase Santayana: "Those who do not remember their past are condemned to repeat their mistakes."

Yet, the drama intensifies. As I write this, manned mainly by U.S. troops, there are war games going on right on Russia's borders in Poland. There are substantial increases in troops and equipment in Poland and the Baltic states. A new ABM system has just been deployed in Romania. Last year the U.S. staged war games called Sea Breeze, and is now sailing war ships and aircraft carriers into the Black Sea seemingly to intentionally provoke Russia and test its patience.

Plus the rhetoric from the U.S. and NATO is becoming even more skewed and provocative. At the recent July 2016 NATO meeting in Warsaw, Russia was declared the major threat to peace and stability in Europe. Of course, no one could point at any aggression on Russia's part, other than the trumped up and discredited accusations of fighting in eastern Ukraine and having invaded and seized control of Crimea. But facts don't discourage western politicians and U.S. media from beating the drums of war, increasing tensions, and risking a major military confrontation. When you wear a white hat, you get to decide who the black hats are.

Frankly, it's shocking what comes out of the mouths of Obama, Joe Biden, John Kerry, Samantha Power, Victoria Nuland, Susan Rice, and other spokespersons for the U.S. government. There is no equivalent that I can see coming from the Russian side. They tend to be restrained, diplomatic, and at least on the public side very respectful and statesmanlike. Obama has in a number of high-visibility public forums made it his personal mission to insult

Vladimir Putin and propagate what are proven lies about Russia. He mocked Putin and Russia in his 2015 State of the Union address. He went before the entire world in a speech at the United Nations and spouted one falsehood after another. If Obama actually believes any of this stuff, then instead of attending foreign policy and intelligence briefings, he must be reading comic books or getting his information from Ted Nugent's website. But to be honest, I've concluded he knows the truth and this propaganda assault is quite intentional.

Just a month before this book was published, Hillary Clinton went off on a rant in an "important foreign policy speech", threatening Russia and making all sorts of unsubstantiated accusations. In this gale of insults and puffery, she again asserted her firm belief that America is "the indispensable nation." Now just stop and think about that. If the U.S. is the indispensable nation, what does that make the other 195? That's right. *Dispensable!* They don't count. America doesn't need you, so if you get in our way, good luck.

The thought of this warmonger becoming president makes me shudder.

Back to Russia ...

Despite the barrage of vituperation and insults from the West, you cannot find one instance of Putin, Foreign Minister Sergey Lavrov, Defense Minister Sergei Shoygu, or any other high official in the ranks of power in Russia, conducting themselves with anything other than courtesy and professionalism.

Frankly, it's often embarrassing to see the way U.S. diplomats swagger around like they're on their way to a barroom brawl in America's Old West. The contrast with Russia's spokespersons is stark and revealing.

Final thoughts ...

It would be one thing if the feud between Obama and Putin were just some school yard scrap between two pubescent boys. But these are the heads of state for two major countries armed to the teeth with nuclear missiles, weighed with almost seven decades of bad blood between them, much of the bad blood alarmingly the product of gross misunderstanding.

The price of more of the same aggravation and contentiousness is at best wasting valuable resources and energy which could be devoted to other mounting crises — climate change, the rapid destruction of the oceans, the spread of antibiotic-resistant disease, desertification of farmland, depletion of water resources throughout the world, increasing risk of widespread famine, the urgent need to secure vast stockpiles of nuclear weapons from access by terrorists — at worst an epic nuclear holocaust which puts the human race in a giant coffin.

Isn't it time to stop the name-calling?

Isn't it time to put away the gang colors?

The black hats and the white hats?

Russia Bad! America Good!

Nothing is that simple.

Unless you're simpleminded.

China

The U.S. has no monopoly on manufacturing fear.

In Japan, the current right wing administration led by Prime Minister Shinjo Abe is promoting its agenda and reinforcing its grip on political power by invoking the threat of Chinese aggression.

Since World War II, a new constitution for Japan — largely written incidentally by the U.S. as victor in the war — specifically precludes Japan from engaging its military, meager as it now is, in anything but defense of the country on its own soil. The particular anti-military clause in the constitution is Article 9.

It is now under assault by the current right wing, nationalistic ruling party, creating a huge public clamor, widespread outrage at even thinking about eliminating this prohibition of war and pursuing a more aggressive military.

How is this happening?

The reason given for needing a military build up is to counter mounting threats from North Korea and China. We'll get to North Korea next but for now let's talk about China.

The right wing in Japan and a forgetful Japanese public apparently sees no irony in their concerns about a "threat from China".

China has never attacked Japan. (Some might claim the Mongol invasions in the 13th Century contradicts this, but this wasn't a markedly Chinese initiative. In fact China proper was also under threat by the Mongol hordes.)

On the other hand, Japan brutally savaged China several times. The most infamous and horrifying example of this is referred to as the Rape of Nanking, a gruesome massacre by the invading Japanese army which occurred over six weeks starting December 13, 1937. It is estimated that as many as 300,000 innocent civilians and disarmed combatants were murdered in cold blood.

And Japan is afraid of China?

Among the major nations of the world, China is among the least militarily aggressive. It attacked Vietnam over border disputes and sovereignty over the Paracel Islands, in what were by standards of major war mere skirmishes.

Compared to the aggressive policies of Japan and the U.S. — both driven by imperial overreach — China's use of its military is trivial.

Japan started World War II, not China. Yes, China like every nation in the world except maybe Bhutan has had some conflicts with other countries. But let's look at some facts. The U.S. for reasons no one can remember now killed up to 3 million Vietnamese. It dropped twice as many bombs on Vietnam, Laos and Cambodia (Laos and Cambodia weren't even officially in the war) as it did in World War II in both Europe and Asia! The U.S. sprayed huge areas of South Vietnam with toxic chemicals, as if the Vietnamese were just insects, not humans. And it wasn't just Vietnam. The U.S. has effectively destroyed Iraq and Libya as functioning nations. Destroyed whole countries!

31

The U.S. has overthrown over thirty governments in the last seven decades, many of them democratically-elected. Not one of these countries had attacked the U.S., meaning this was unprovoked aggression.

America's relationship with China certainly isn't lily white either.

It goes back aways. Does the Boxer Rebellion ring a bell?

I was taught in high school world history class that this was an uprising against the West in China, specifically Beijing, which illegally seized power from the legitimate authorities, and was subsequently put down by Western powers with the help of Japan, to restore the proper order. It was a turn-of-the-20th Century example of the enlightened West fighting the evil of terrorism in a nation we held dear to us because of our mutually-beneficial trade relations.

The truth is that China had been the victim of a vast opium trade, promoted by the West over several decades, which resulted in massive addiction and effectively a subjugation of China to economic manipulation and control by the West. The Boxer Rebellion was an attempt to reclaim the country from foreign control and eliminate the scourge of opium addiction and the resulting disintegration of Chinese society. The U.S. deployed war ships and marines giving initial support to the British to fight the Chinese. Eventually, Germany, Russia, Austria, Japan, and Australia joined in to suppress the rebellion. The U.S. was thus partially responsible for attacking those in China who were battling colonial tyranny by the West and Japan.

Xi Jinping, the current president of the People's Republic of China, as many other embittered Chinese scholars likewise do, refers to this era of addiction and enslavement as the Century of Humiliation. He has vowed to never allow China to be subjected to such disrespect again. This is what drives his foreign policy and what our historically-ignorant politicos view as his "confrontational" policies and recalcitrance with the U.S.

China-bashers in the U.S. need to get some perspective before they accuse China of being aggressive. That would start by Americans take a long hard look at themselves in the mirror.

Many Americans also accuse China of trying to take over the world. Are these the same people who handed over huge sectors of our manufacturing to China, gutting America's own industrial base? Are these the same brilliant economic minds who rely on China to keep America solvent (China currently holds $1.243 trillion in U.S. treasuries)? Yes, China is expanding its presence across the globe. But China's economic ascendency didn't require military might. Much of it directly resulted from the greed of U.S. corporate CEOs and the ingenious economic direction of American economists and government officials putting the interests of Wall Street and multinational corporations above the welfare of the nation. Much of it resulted from China's constructive and respectful policies, its win-win approach to working with other countries, it's desire to build business partnerships, not military alliances.

Some accuse China of having an abysmal human rights record, of abusing its citizens and limiting their freedom.

To begin with, what business is that of America? It seems to me that it's a matter that the Chinese people first and foremost need to deal with. Do you see millions of oppressed Chinese begging America to come to their aid? Besides, if we're so principled, why do we do so much business with China? If we feel so bad about working conditions in China, why is it we have no problem with our iPhones, sneakers, toys, clothing, appliances, games, etc. being manufactured by these same oppressed Chinese laborers, just so that we can save a few bucks on them at Walmart? Smells like a big steaming pile of hypocrisy to me.

More importantly, since when does the kettle get to call the frying pan black? China may not have a sterling human rights record. But just look at the U.S. America has been caught red-handed illegally spying on its citizens, conducting 24/7 unconstitutional invasions of our privacy. It prosecutes whistleblowers and even journalists, contrary to the letter and spirit of the U.S. Constitution. The U.S. has the highest incarceration rate in the world. The imprisoned are disproportionately people of color. Police kill unarmed citizens in America at an alarming rate. Unarmed black people are five times as likely to be killed as unarmed white people.

Apparently, freedom in America is freedom to be spied on 24/7, the freedom to go to prison, the freedom to read state-sponsored propaganda, the freedom to complain about how horrific other countries treat their citizens, the freedom to get shot by the police, the freedom if possible to be white.

I don't want to be simplistic here. But frankly, much of the China bashing comes down to a mouthful of sour grapes. We demonized China for decades over their communist ideology, where the state owned and controlled every aspect of life. Prompted by a degree of failure of this narrow system, China liberalized and introduced elements of capitalism. While politically it's still at core a communist country, the economy is very much a hybrid affair. There are fast food restaurants, Pizza Hut and McDonald's, in Beijing. They have a stock market. They took the best from the west and kept the most productive elements of their own economic planning and are now thriving.

China may indeed be taking over the world. But they're doing it fair and square, non-violently, comfortably within the parameters we hold ourselves to. But while America's economy is faltering, right now growing a mere 1.1% per year, China's is currently growing at 6.7% annually. As recent as 2007, China's GDP growth rate was over 14%. China surpassed the powerhouse

Japanese economy to become the second largest in the world, and is on its way to overtaking the U.S. to become number one.

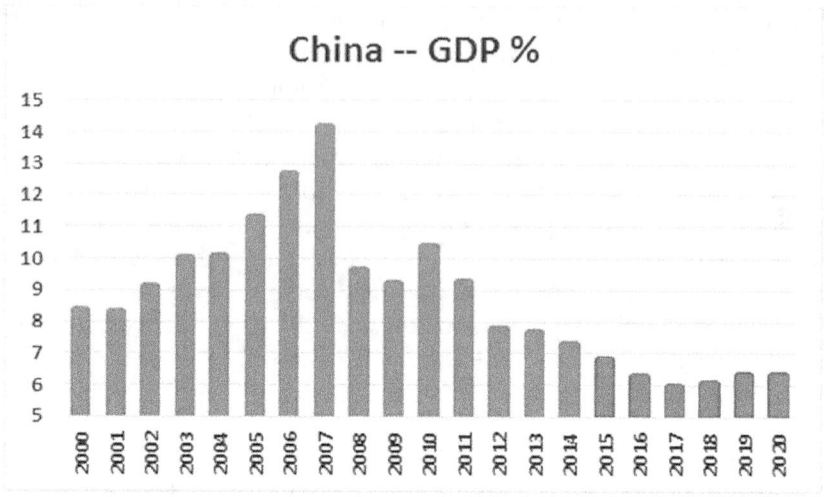

China -- GDP %

What is America proposing to do about it?

We have a one-size-fits-all approach to dealing with competition:

Confront, destabilize, overthrow. If that doesn't work, start a war.

Free and fair competition is for sissies. Bring out the bombs!

But there's something to consider here.

Maybe inside the Washington DC bubble, the self-proclaimed rulers of the Universe feel comfortable immersing themselves in comic book delusions of easy conquest. Let's hope and pray these daydreamers come to their senses. China has been around for 4,000 years. They have some of the most advanced weaponry on the planet. China has 260 nuclear weapons. They currently have the largest active military in the world — 2,333,000 soldiers in uniform.

China is not Grenada or Panama.

China does not want war. But they will defend themselves.

American citizens need to wake up and get their crazed, saber-rattling politicos under control before it's too late.

North Korea

It's difficult to keep a clear head when it comes to North Korea.

Sometimes looking at their leader, Kim Jong-un, it's all we can do to keep a straight face. He's juvenile, full of himself, impulsive, has a ridiculous hairdo, struts around without irony like Charlie Chaplin.

We could dismiss him as a ridiculous and harmless fool, except from all outward appearances he's crazy, and North Korea possesses at least a handful of nuclear weapons. Kim Jong-un is ruthless at home, executing anyone who

34

looks at him cross-eyed. In terms of the rest of the world, he never misses an opportunity to boast, threaten, rant like a temperamental child.

Regardless, as I said previously, before making snap judgments which only further muddy an understanding of behavior, it's good to know a little history. In this case, it will give rise to glimpses of a shrewd, sporadic sanity in Kim Jong-un's seemingly unhinged modus operandi — a method in at least some of the madness — something we might be able to build on and use constructively.

Here is some necessary background, a short summary culled from an excellent article by Caleb Maupin that appeared in Global Research titled "Korea: The Dangerous Tone of US Media. Why is the Korean Nation Divided?" ...

> "When the Second World War ended in 1945, the northern half of the Korean Peninsula had been liberated by Soviet troops. The southern half of the Korean Peninsula soon became occupied by US troops. In the northern part of the country, the major anti-Japanese resistance political parties — including communists, Social Democrats, agrarian revolutionaries, Christians, and many others — merged in 1948 to form the Korean Workers Party."

Mind you, Korea had been under the oppressive thumb of Japan since 1910, subjected to horrifying cruelty and humiliation. The end of the war meant the end of Japanese subjugation. There was great hope and enthusiasm about beginning to function again as a free and independent nation.

It was understood that there would be free elections across the entire peninsula, a new constitution would be written and a government formed.

> "However, in the southern half of the Peninsula, a military dictatorship was established. Syngman Rhee seized power and violently suppressed all opposition. The Rhee dictatorship was openly supported by the United States. Thousands of US troops poured into the country to prop up the military regime ....

> "In response to US military occupation of the southern half of Korea, the canceling of free elections, and the slaughter of innocent Korean civilians by US troops, the Democratic People's Republic of Korea (DPRK) based in the northern territories of the peninsula, sent forces into the south, hoping to reunify the country and drive out US troops.

> "The response to the attempted reunification was the horrific United Nations 'police action,' more commonly known as the

Korean War. The United States bombed every building above one story tall in the northern half of the country. Dams were bombed in order to cause mass flooding of civilian areas. Between 3 and 4 million Koreans were killed.

"An armistice was declared in 1953 — but the United States never signed a peace treaty, as was agreed upon. The Korean War technically never ended, and the United States has not even recognized the DPRK as a legitimate government."

Calling the 'police action' horrific is not an exaggeration. Toward the end of the bombing campaign by America, bombers were returning *with* their bombs, complaining there was nothing left to destroy. The late Air Force General Curtis Lemay, who headed up the Strategic Air Command at the time, claimed with little remorse that the U.S. killed 20% of the population!

Again we have a country whose "paranoid" behavior was shaped by its prior destruction at the hands of an invader: Russia by Nazi Germany, China by the West partnered with Japan in the Century of Humiliation, now North Korea leveled by the brutality of the U.S. during the Korean War, a barbaric slaughter that many have judged as a war crime.

The U.S. almost 65 years later continues its standoff with North Korea. Just recently the U.S. announced it will be installing the THAAD ABM system in South Korea, a move that has incensed North Korea and resulted in condemnation by both Russia and China, both of whom believe they are the actual targets, that pointing the finger at North Korea is just a ruse.

As crazy as Kim Jong-un is, the lessons of recent history have not been lost on him. We destroyed Libya after it became clear that *did not have* and they were no longer attempting to obtain nuclear weapons. Similarly we destroyed Iraq because they *did not have* weapons of mass destruction — we knew they didn't and British and U.S. intelligence was "fixed" around the prior decision to go to war — knowing that without nuclear weapons, the scope of their retaliation would be limited.

In light of this, Kim Jong-un actually makes sense. He brags about North Korea's nuclear weapons, most recently the unlikely prospect that they have a hydrogen bomb, all focused on dissuading the U.S. from destroying it again. If he's bluffing, it's most assuredly a risky ploy. But what else does he have?

North Korea claims it just wants a guarantee in writing that it will not be attacked by the U.S. or South Korea or any combination or coalition of countries the U.S. cobbles together for the occasion.

We could start by listening to what North Korea has to say, containing it with the cooperation of just about every other country in the world, calling its bluff by actually offering to sign a permanent peace treaty. Just signing the original treaty the U.S. has refused to sign since 1953 would do the trick.

What does the U.S. have to lose here?

Maybe this simple gesture is all it would take to calm down Kim Jong-un and start to defuse this volatile confrontation. We won't know until we try.

One thing is certain. We don't need an arsenal of over 7,000 nuclear weapons, the largest air force and navy since the dawn of civilization, to stand down North Korea's four nuclear weapons and the slingshot or whatever they'll use to threaten to rain devastation on the rest of the planet.

A little common sense and diplomacy would go a long way here.

ISIS, al Qaeda, Terrorism

How is America doing in the War on Terrorism?

The logic of this fight has turned out to be a cruel joke.

Let's face the facts …

The more terrorists we kill, the more the terrorists multiply.

Nothing is working. In fact, not only is it not working, it has trapped America in a death spiral. While the terrorists can't claim a dramatic victory on the field of battle, neither can we. For one thing, there pretty much isn't a field of battle, not in the traditional military sense. There isn't an opposing military either. There are fighters, jihadists, huge numbers of men armed to the teeth with highly lethal, often with the best, most modern weapons. There are leaders but there are no formal institutions, there are pockets and cells of activity but no capitals, no national framework, no formal organization offering targets for our familiar way of fighting wars. We might never lose the War on Terror, but we may never win it either.

We pursue our War on Terror with characteristic American can-do optimism, but we just get sucked deeper and deeper into the conflict.

Yes, we are prisoners of a self-inflicted death spiral. Who are the victims? It's us. It's our democracy. It's our peace of mind. It's our constitutional values, our rights of privacy, our freedom. Yes, our freedom. The thing that always comes up first when we say we need to go out there and do battle, bomb some country, assassinate someone with a Predator drone, send in the Navy Seals for some deep penetration and target elimination. It's to protect our freedom. Go Team America!

Is there anyone out there who feels as free as he or she did before all of this started? With the 24/7 surveillance, the overbearing presence of a highly militarized police, with the constant dread of being under attack, "terrorists" lurking behind every tree and household appliance.

Are you feeling the freedom, folks? I'm not.

Yet, what do we do? What does our government do? How do we get out from under this oppressive doomsday storm cloud and move on?

Do I have to answer that? We watch as we keep doing the same things, the same way that hasn't and isn't working, using the same formulas, the same mentality and strategies and weapons which are making us less safe, making the rest of the world less safe, turning greater swaths of territory into incipient battlefields where terrorists can fight their war and define success on their own terms. Yet ...

Our imagination-challenged politicos trot out and repeat the same mantras.

More bombing.

More drones.

More nuclear weapons.

More military hardware.

ISIS. What good are nuclear weapons against a renegade band of brutal beheaders wandering in the desert? How will an F-35 protect us from lunatics who set off bombs at marathons or in a crowded movie theater here at home?

Al Qaeda. Al Nusra.

How are we going to stop them?

OMG! Nothing works!

They're everywhere!

At least, that's what the public has been taught to think.

That's how the public has been trained to react. *Trained!*

And like good little trained monkeys, we stand on our heads, squeal and mug, shimmy and shake when the organ grinder turns the crank.

Instead of being the big bad tough Americans we always claim we are, we act like frightened children, cowering and whining for daddy to protect us.

Yeah ... we're really tough.

America? Home of the brave?

Hardly.

Certainly not under the deluge of scare mongering lies.

We are a nation of fear.

We live fear. We breathe fear. We ...

Wait! I just got an idea!

How about a dose of reality for a change?

How about some perspective?

Here are the facts ...

Since 9/11, a grand total of 45 Americans have been killed by terrorists.

I'm not counting the attack on the gay club in Orlando. This was not an act of terrorism but a mass shooting by a home-grown, homophobic lunatic.

So it's 45. That's about 3 per year.

I'm not going to callously marginalize the tragedy of 45 deaths. All these were people who had families, friends, dreams for the future. Each one is a sad example of what it means to live in a dangerous world.

But think about it ... only 45 people have been killed by terrorists in the last 15 years.

Now some reality ...

Last year alone, there were 16,121 HOMICIDES. 11,208 of those were people killed by firearms! That more than one gun killing PER HOUR!

How about inebriated slaughter on our nation's roads: Every 51 minutes in America, someone is killed by drunk driving. Almost 11,000 a year!

Last year 1,658,370 new cancer cases were diagnosed. 589,430 people died of cancer! That's 1,615 A DAY! 67 people PER HOUR!

Over 102,000 people die EVERY YEAR from hospital associated infections — by the time you finish this section, two people will have died from filthy medical facilities.

Get this: Last year 251,454 died because of medical error! Yes, you read that correctly. Almost 700 people die EVERY DAY because of misdiagnosis, faulty administering of recommended medications and procedures, error in reading medical charts. *"Golly gee. I'm sorry. It said 20.00 cc. I was sure it was 2000 cc. Oops! Can you notify the family of the deceased for me?"*

I could go on and on. But this offers some perspective: Rare as it is to be electrocuted in a storm, you are *seventeen times more likely* to get killed by lightning than by a terrorist.

Let's cut to the chase ...

Since 2001, the U.S. has spent over $3 trillion on the War on Terror.

That's *$3 trillion* with a 't'.

For $3 trillion we could have outfitted everyone with bulletproof vests, cured cancer, put breathalyzer shut-offs on every single car to keep drunks from getting behind the wheel, disinfected every hospital in America, outfitted every single American with a lighting rod, and probably had some money left over to train nurses and doctors how to read a medical chart.

What's going on in this country ... home of the *brave*, land of the free?

Oh yes, indeed we are free. Free to wake up frightened, go to bed frightened, live every moment frightened because ... HELP! THERE ARE TERRORISTS LURKING EVERYWHERE! They hate us, they hate our freedoms, they want to chop off our heads, rape our women!

I agree about one thing for sure ...

We *should* be afraid.

We *should* be afraid that our priorities are completely whack and that our government is overrun by self-serving lunatics, at the beck and call of our equally crazed out-of-control military!

Here are a few questions we can ask ourselves to get some perspective ...

How many of you have known a friend, relative or neighbor who has died of cancer?

How many of you have known someone who has a family member killed by a drunk driver?

How many of you live in a community where someone was murdered?

Contrast your answers with ...

How many of you know someone who was attacked by a Muslim?

How many of you know someone who was killed by a terrorist?

How many of you has seen a terrorist anywhere in your town?

Folks … *the War On Terror is a fraud!*

It's just a cash cow for our bloated military-industrial complex.

All I can suggest is this: Every time one of the fear peddlers comes on TV and shows you guys in ski masks and tell you to hide under your bed … GET A GRIP!

You are more likely to get hit by a bus while you're under your bed, than be attacked by a terrorist while standing at a bus stop.

Here, ladies and gentlemen, is my prediction for each and every one of you this coming year.

Ready?

You <u>WILL</u> <u>NOT</u> <u>BE</u> <u>KILLED</u> by ISIS or al Qaeda or al Nusra or by Boko Haram guerillas.

Actually, you're much more likely to be killed by your local police.

So let's stop the fear mongering.

Let's turn off the money spigots and save ourselves from annihilation.

Let's stop making enemies by declaring everyone is an enemy.

Start Making Sense

Follow the Mantra

There are some bad people in the world.
There are threats which need to be addressed.
But all of the fear and trembling makes no sense.
The boogeymen are bogus.
The wars of the recent past are a fraud.
The coming wars are a fraud.
The War on Terrorism is a fraud.
But that leaves us with a big problem ...

How do we explain the incessant harangues against Putin, Russia, Iran, China, North Korea, the constant fear mongering about ISIS?

It's actually ridiculously easy to answer that question. It's not a secret. There's not some dark, mysterious cabal behind it. Its proponents have not sworn on the blood of their children to secrecy. In fact, they have proudly and brazenly written about it in journals, newspapers, magazines, and even on the internet!

It has to do with a geopolitical world view but in the final analysis, to get to the absolute bottom of it all — as they always say — just follow the money.

First, we need to look at a bit of theory, the world view part.

There's no need to panic because there's nothing complicated about any of this. And the really good news is that it explains just about everything. At least it sheds some light on why the U.S. is doing the fatally stupid things it's doing right now.

The Wolfowitz Doctrine

Paul Wolfowitz has turned out to be one of the most dangerous men to have ever served in high office, to both America and the rest of the world.

The real problem with policymakers of his ilk is that on the surface they appear reasonable and seem to make sense. That is, they cloak their ideas in a framework that appears cogitative, rational, logical, even laudable.

The Wolfowitz Doctrine was a landmark policy embedded in Defense Planning Guidance recommendations issued in 1992, when Wolfowitz was Under Secretary of Defense for Policy. As Wikipedia says, "The document was widely criticized as imperialist as the document outlined a policy of unilateralism and pre-emptive military action to suppress potential threats from other nations and prevent any other nation from rising to superpower status." This paradigm-shifting proposal in short order established the tone and substance for America's expression — and abuse — of power over the subsequent two-and-a-half decades:

> *"Our first objective is to prevent the re-emergence of a new rival, either on the territory of the former Soviet Union or elsewhere, that poses a threat on the order of that posed formerly by the Soviet Union. This is a dominant consideration underlying the new regional defense strategy and requires that we endeavor to prevent any hostile power from dominating a region whose resources would, under consolidated control, be sufficient to generate global power."*

What's wrong with this?

Basically two things.

First, it ignores the fact that there are another 195 nations in the world which host almost 96% of the world's population, and these countries have credible priorities and agendas as well.

Second, perhaps more fatefully, it potentially puts the U.S. at odds with every other country on the planet. Cooperation is reduced to vassalage to the U.S., assuring that in almost every instance it will be impossible. Many if not all other countries do not want to bow down to America, as self-appointed ruler of the globe. Our arrogance and sense of entitlement — exceptionalism — will guarantee that we will always be at war. At least until we come to our senses and accept our place beside others in a community of nations, not as the bullying emperor. Bear in mind that when we call ourselves "exceptional", it suggests that all others are unexceptional, less worthy, not to be taken seriously. Their priorities and needs are secondary to those of *exceptional America*. Can you see where this is certain to create resentment?

Keep in mind what "to prevent the re-emergence of a new rival" implies. Effectively, if a nation appears to be gaining enough stature to challenge the U.S., it becomes the target of all sorts of destructive machinations: manipulation of their currency, embargoes, economic sanctions, crippling of their economy, infiltration by agitators. They become either victims of proxy terrorism, or direct military aggression by the U.S.

The current sanctions regime against Russia is a perfect example of counter-productive posturing which has only produced enormous ill will and distrust, created unnecessary hardship, and has done nothing to foster better understanding and a more stable, harmonious relationship between countries.

Bullies become targets, and we are now increasingly in the crosshairs of more and more nations who don't buy into our chest-beating bluster and intimidation. Our arrogant embrace of the Wolfowitz Doctrine is proving to be self-sabotaging and dangerous. Yet it persists, draining energy and resources, wasting valuable time, depleting what good will the U.S. still enjoys.

There are many enormous challenges facing the world right now. Some of them literally threaten the survival of the human race. While these challenges go unaddressed the U.S. preoccupies itself battling for preeminence, jockeying for position, fending and defending is energy and time which is diverted from the real crises we face:

- Climate change.
- Resource depletion.
- Potential for nuclear war and the annihilation of the planet.
- Desertification of shrinking tracts of farm land.
- Diminishing fresh water supplies.
- Acidification of the oceans and overfishing.
- Increasing risk of famine.
- Antibiotic-resistant diseases.
- Accelerating species extinction.
- Human trafficking and enslavement.

It's not like we don't have a choice. It's not like it's America's being the world's undisputed, undefeated champion of all of mankind is some divinely ordained holy writ, and that's the only way the world can possibly function.

America does not have to play this game.

More importantly, we as citizens do not have to cheer this on.

This insanity has already cost good, decent, hard-working American taxpayers $4.82 trillion. Empire and war are expensive.

Enough is enough!

Zbigniew Brzezinski and the Grand Chessboard

The Wolfowitz Doctrine was paralleled by the highly influential geo-political analysis of Zbigniew Brzezinski, National Security Advisor under President Jimmy Carter. His doctrine was codified in his landmark book *The Grand Chessboard: American Primacy And Its Geostrategic Imperatives*, providing a comprehensive theoretical framework justifying U.S. supremacy and world domination.

Here is a key passage which embraces the fundamental thrust of the book, outlining where the application of American power is paramount:

> *"How America 'manages' Eurasia is critical. A power that dominates Eurasia would control two of the world's three most advanced and economically productive regions. A mere glance at the map also suggests that control over Eurasia would almost automatically entail Africa's subordination, rendering the Western Hemisphere and Oceania geopolitically peripheral to the world's central continent. About 75 per cent of the world's*

people live in Eurasia, and most of the world's physical wealth is there as well, both in its enterprises and underneath its soil. Eurasia accounts for about three-fourths of the world's known energy resources."

Eurasia? Doesn't this include among others Russia and China?
Yes, we must *dominate Eurasia* to control the world.
Is there any question what gives rise to our past and present follies?
Why did we destroy Vietnam and kill 3 million of its people?
Why do we still have 54,000 troops in Japan?
Why do we still have almost 30,000 troops in South Korea?
Why do we still have over 25,000 troops in Europe?
Why have we encircled Russia and China with military bases and with promises of more to come?

We must *dominate Eurasia* to control the world!
Note that this entire proposition, this sweeping world view, regardless of how erudite and persuasive it appears to be, mimics the colonialism of Great Britain and other European powers, empires all of which eventually self-destructed. It is a pattern of thinking which dismisses and ignores entirely the possibility of all nations accepting their respective positions in a balanced environment of harmonious engagement and cooperation. It is based purely on conquest. It is a foundation for perpetual war.

This is the route which America has taken, failing to learn the lessons of history or recognizing the limits of its own power. It's pure neocolonialism, i.e. conquer, enslave, plunder.

It may have new appealing spin and trappings. Free trade, responsibility to protect, promoting democracy.

But it's just putting a new façade on an old game.

Conquer, enslave, plunder.

Interestingly, even Brzezinski — the fierce attack dog and darling of the neocon war hawks who live and breathe American exceptionalism — has just recently expressed second thoughts about his "vision" for Pax Americana.

Waking up is hard to do.

Better late than never.

The Project for the New American Century (PNAC)

Imposing U.S. hegemony on the world got a major shot of boosterism from an organization co-founded in 1997 under the "Chairmanship of William Kristol, former Chief of Staff to Vice President Dan Quale during the Presidency of George Bush Senior," and Robert Kagan, who currently is "a senior associate of the Carnegie Endowment for International Peace" and adviser to President Obama. This was the Project for the New American Century. It's agenda was simply to push America to a position of power and preeminence in the world. This required dramatically increasing the military might of the U.S., hence vastly increasing the military budget. It was the influence of the PNAC and its founding signatories which spelled a death warrant for the peace dividend promised in 1992. Justification for the resulting explosion of the DOD budget was found by identifying threats to our national security wherever possible. If real threats were not convincing, then exaggerating what was available became the order of the day. If threats were not available, then new ones were created by intimidation and bullying. A list of governments to be overthrown was drawn up. If overthrow by subterfuge didn't work, then bombing them into submission always works.

The list should sound familiar: Afghanistan, Iraq, Syria, Lebanon, Libya, Somalia, Sudan, Iran.

This represented — and unfortunately still represents — the thinking of allegedly the "best minds" in the military/political establishment. Attack, bomb, destroy, kill. "Many other members have been long-time fixtures in the U.S. military establishment or Cold War 'strategic studies,' including Elliott Abrams, Dick Cheney, Paula Dobriansky, Aaron Friedberg, Frank Gaffney, Fred C. Ikle, Peter W. Rodman, Stephen P. Rosen, Henry S. Rowen, Donald H. Rumsfeld, John R. Bolton, Vin Weber, and Paul Dundes Wolfowitz."

These are the architects of many of our ongoing disasters.

This is the rogues gallery that put America on the path of perpetual war.

These are first among the ideologues who are bankrupting our nation.

These are the individuals who laid the foundation for the fraud perpetrated on the American public — the theft of over $4.82 trillion of our tax dollars to pursue delusions of world empire.

Bad ideas can be very expensive.

Follow the Money

No ideology or set of operating principles operates in a vacuum.

Social, theological, historical, and most importantly, economic factors create an environment in which ideological principles, and the specific guidelines which grow out of them, either thrive or perish. In America we can say with confidence that it is FIRE community — finance, investment, real estate — which weighs in decisively on what ideology prevails in directing the course of our country. In other words, "if it pays it plays."

We have just looked at three ways our current pursuit of world domination and the consequent emphasis on military power and conquest were framed, thus becoming the de facto "bible" for defining our relationship with the rest of the world. That this approach is the source of phenomenal enrichment of the tiny class of wealthy oligarchs who already own and control much of America's wealth, is no accident.

War . . . what is it good for? . . . Profits!

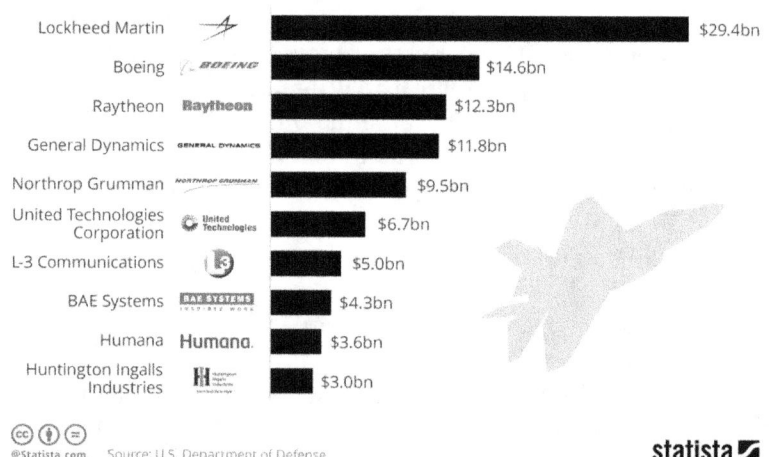

America's Biggest Defense Contractors
U.S. Department of Defense expenditure with contractors in 2015

Lockheed Martin	$29.4bn
Boeing	$14.6bn
Raytheon	$12.3bn
General Dynamics	$11.8bn
Northrop Grumman	$9.5bn
United Technologies Corporation	$6.7bn
L-3 Communications	$5.0bn
BAE Systems	$4.3bn
Humana	$3.6bn
Huntington Ingalls Industries	$3.0bn

@Statista_com   Source: U.S. Department of Defense

statista

War . . . war . . . war.

So many wars. So little time.

Who remembers the great song released in 1970 by R&B singer Edwin Starr, called "War"?:

War, huh, yeah.
What is it good for?
Absolutely nothing
Uh-huh. War, huh, yeah ...

Absolutely nothing?

While the lyrics were great and an inspiration to the anti-war movement — which was railing against the Vietnam War at the time — unfortunately war *is* good for something.

Profits!

The U.S. is the biggest exporter of weapons in the world.

One great thing about all of this killing hardware, much of which will ultimately be turned around and used against *us* by terrorists or former-friends now-enemies: We can proudly point to the label on each and every weapon, one which isn't seen very often these days on much of anything else ...

MADE IN AMERICA!

My heart swells with such patriotic pride to know that we're applying so much American ingenuity and hard work to keeping our corporate defense contractors and their CEOs rolling in the dough.

Gosh ... I'm getting all teary-eyed!

Despite my crocodile tears, there is something to *always* keep in mind when it comes to war.

War is always about money.

Money for corporations.

Money for investment banks.

Money for the already filthy rich.

And when it comes to making money, these folks will tell you anything you want to hear to get you to fight the wars, die for your country, fork over your hard-earned tax dollars, sacrifice what you have coming to you, so they can make a buck.

Billions and billions and billions of bucks!

The Bully on the Block

Isn't it about time to stop this ugly business?

Isn't it about time to stop this ugly business of meddling in other countries affairs and overthrowing governments?

First there's the really blatant interference, the hard-core meddling, as in dropping bombs:

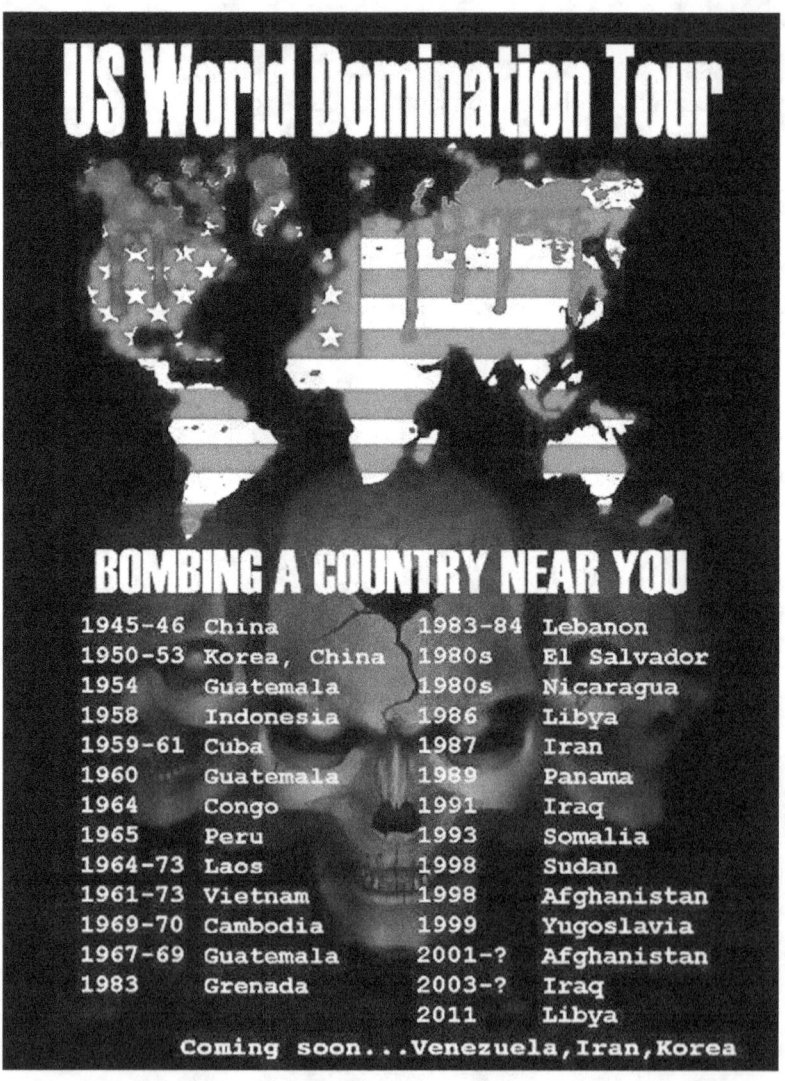

By the way, none of these countries attacked us. Not a single one. Predictably there were all sorts of reasons for bombing them.

Moving along, here's the short list of U.S.-backed coups over just the past seven-plus decades:

Syria 1949.

Iran 1953.

Guatemala 1954.

Tibet 1955-1970s.

Indonesia 1958.

Cuba 1959.

Iraq 1960-1963.

Democratic Republic of the Congo 1960-1965.

Dominican Republic 1962.

Guatemala 1963.

South Vietnam 1963.

Brazil 1964.

Ghana 1966.

Chile 1970-1973.

Argentina 1976.

Afghanistan 1979-1989.

Turkey 1980.

Poland 1980-1989.

Ecuador 1981.

Panama 1981.

Nicaragua 1981-1990.

Grenada 1983.

Haiti 1991.

Iraq 1992-1996.

Venezuela 2002.

Haiti 2004.

Iran 2005-present.

Honduras 2009.

Libya 2011.

Syria 2012-present.

Ukraine 2014.

Moreover, it's no secret that we're at it again right now with Venezuela and Brazil, and a poorly-kept secret that Russia, Ecuador, Uruguay, Bolivia, probably another shot at Cuba, and (you heard it here first) Kyrgyzstan, are also in the queue.

Here's what has become the fundamental tenets of America's current foreign policy:

1. We make the rules.
2. Winning is everything.
3. Preemptive attacks are awesome.
4. All is fair because we say it is.
5. Playing nice is for wimps.

When other nations see NGOs like NED (National Endowment for Democracy) or USAID (United States Agency for International Development) come knocking on the door saying, *"We're just here to help!"*, they understandably either run the other way in complete panic, or more frighteningly — as in the case of Russia — put their entire nuclear arsenal and ground troops on hair-trigger high alert.

Thus I predict, with 100% confidence, that the days of U.S. meddling, both overt and covert bullying, overthrowing foreign governments, especially the one-size-fits-all destructive military deployments, are numbered — except for maybe just one more very epic, history-making coup.

That will be …

Regime change in Washington DC itself.

At the rate things are going, we might not have to wait that long.

R2P = L2K

War by any other name is war.

Killing is killing.

We know that. So our leaders are always coming up with new, alluring ways to justify war. They appeal to our better nature in order for us to rationalize and justify expressing our savagery and bloodlust.

The latest gambit for aggression is R2P … responsibility to protect.

Robert Scheer at Truthdig treats us to an oft-recurring refrain in his impassioned pleas for sanity and common sense. I've heard it any number of times in the many informative, fascinating interviews I've heard of this brilliant, inspiring journalist. Here it is ...

"What happens to these people?"

Indeed!

What happened to Colin Powell?

He ruined a sterling reputation and destroyed his historical legacy by lying at the U.N. — with the whole world watching — about WMDs in Iraq. Hundreds of thousands of people died so he could make his boss, George W. Bush, proud of him. Tragic on so many levels.

Here's a good one: What happened to Dick Cheney?

This is the man behind the curtain, personally responsible for more chaos and carnage than anyone since Richard Nixon murdered 3 million people in Vietnam and Cambodia. What follows is truly mind-boggling! This is what he said in 1994 on why the U.S. *should not* have invaded Iraq and taken down Saddam Hussein during Desert Shield, the first Gulf War in Iraq:

> "Because if we had gone to Baghdad we would have been all alone. There wouldn't have been anybody else with us. It would have been a U.S. occupation of Iraq. None of the Arab forces that were willing to fight with us in Kuwait were willing to invade Iraq. Once you got to Iraq and took it over and took down Saddam Hussein's government, then what are you going to put in its place? That's a very volatile part of the world. And if you take down the central government in Iraq, you could easily end up seeing pieces of Iraq fly off. Part of it the Syrians would like to have, the west. Part of eastern Iraq the Iranians would like to claim. Fought over for eight years. In the north, you've got the Kurds. And if the Kurds spin loose and join with Kurds in Turkey, then you threaten the territorial integrity of Turkey. It's a quagmire if you go that far and try to take over Iraq."

Okay, Cheney is a psychopath. So we can't expect consistency, much less common sense. You still have to wonder, in 2003 when he pushed America to "go to Baghdad", did he once think about what he said back in 1994?

Moving on ... what happened to Samantha Power?

She is an example of someone who has truly made the ugly and unmitigated transition to the dark side.

She wrote a book on the "responsibility to protect" or R2P, as the convenient acronym goes. The widely-acclaimed book was called *A Problem from Hell: America and the Age of Genocide*, and it won a Pulitzer Prize.

However, this once noble framework and call for responsible, moral action is now the neocon public relations weapon of choice to bomb and destroy any country that has the audacity to disagree with America's corporate imperial ambitions. Power herself has become a bloodthirsty neocon warmonger, who rails incessantly at any national leader or country who stands in the way of America's ruinous march to world hegemony.

R2P now equals L2K — license to kill.

"What happens to these people?"

I think I can answer that but I'm not going to waste my time. Because ...

You know what?

I don't really care what happens to any of these people. Not any more than I care exactly how a dog contracted rabies. When the animal is frothing at the mouth, howling, leaping in the air, snapping at everything in sight, completely out of its mind and posing a danger to everyone — children, old folks, anyone innocently strolling by — there's only one immediate concern, and one sensible thing to do. We need to take action before someone gets hurt.

I'm not proposing shooting these people. But they do need to be isolated before they do any more harm to others. They need to be called out, driven out, shut out, exiled from public life. They must be removed from positions of power <u>before</u> <u>anyone</u> <u>else</u> <u>gets</u> <u>hurt</u>.

"What happens to these people?"

I know what *should* happen to them.

No more pulling punches. No more political correctness or obsequious politeness.

We don't behead here in America. But we certainly do eviscerate public figures — vilify and assassinate them in the public forums, smear and quarantine them, ridicule and demonize them personally, mock and marginalize their messages. Usually it's the good decent ones, citizens and public servants who take their duty to their country seriously and are guided by genuine moral concerns and driven by selfless and magnanimous agendas. People like Don Siegelman, Edward Snowden, Dennis Kucinich, Chelsea Manning, John Kiriakou.

Time to turn the tables and call out the real enemies of America.

These people have made a sham of what this country stands for, lie and deceive the citizenry about the real agenda behind their faux-noble ideas, rationalize and obfuscate the horrifying consequences of their actions.

Yes, we'll start with Samantha Power. Her book, brimming with noble intentions, has morphed into a foreign policy brimming with lethal weapons. She truly is a traitor to both herself and us.

We should show no more mercy toward her than she and her homicidal accomplices have shown the hundreds of thousands they've murdered, in the name of "responsibility to protect".

There should be no safe haven. Wherever this violent, disingenuous shrew appears publicly — and even where possible privately — everyone should be reminded this woman is a murderer and a war criminal. When the outcries and collective revulsion sufficiently builds and she is rendered totally ineffective and discredited, she will be toppled from her pulpit at the United Nations — she is currently United States Ambassador to the U.N. — and the chances of survival for those who she now "protects" will be increased exponentially.

Rot in Hell Samantha Power! You've killed enough people.

Make snuff movies or become a mercenary sniper.

Either is a perfect match for your CV.

The Race to a Vanishing Point

The writing is on the wall. BIG writing!

The U.S. has again unleashed forces it cannot control, to obtain some perceived geopolitical advantage, and give itself some edge in the grand game of chess, played on an immense, impersonal macro-cosmic scale — which ignores individual tragedy, human suffering, destruction of peoples and cultures, the wholesale slaughter of innocent civilians — gradually edging the world toward the ultimate confrontation, the really *big one*, where we get to see what comes out of the other end of a nuclear confrontation.

We obviously learned nothing from our original meddling in Afghanistan, which produced Osama bin Laden and al Qaeda; our meddling in Iran, which produced the current regime we are still trying to dominate; our meddling and war with Iraq, which now has resulted in ISIS; our meddling and destruction of Libya, which now has the country in shambles and has helped spread chaos and carnage across the Middle East and northern Africa.

53

We just *had to meddle even more*, and create the current crisis in Ukraine by toppling the democratically-elected government there, then installing a fierce, racist, ultra-nationalistic "pro-Western" puppet regime which will ultimately put us eyeball-to-eyeball with Russia, a world power armed to the teeth with nuclear missiles.

David Swanson points out in an excellent article in OpEdNews called "Public Didn't See Last Two World Wars Coming Either" that prior to both World War I and World War II, the public remained clueless as to the onset of major conflict. This despite the fact that all the alarms, signals and flags were in plain sight, huge glaring signs that war was where things were inevitably heading. This despite concerned men and women, keen observers, highly visible pundits and scholars — though admittedly they were in the minority and fatefully shouted down by the usual crowd of bombastic exceptionalists and grinning fools — issuing grave and sober warnings, dire and thoughtful forecasts, based on sound and knowledgeable analysis, that the world was marching toward a disaster.

Similarly, the evidence is right before us, big pieces of a straightforward puzzle, which even the most simple-minded dolt could assemble into the frightening picture it is. The insensitive, reckless, aggressive policies of the U.S. are precipitating World War III.

History has dramatically demonstrated that in the heat of major conflict, cooler heads *never* prevail. This coming war could and probably will go nuclear.

There is, of course, every reason to be concerned about putting food on the table, seeing our kids off to school, showing up for work, keeping the house and yard looking nice, making our homes comfortable for ourselves and those we love.

But there's even more reason for preserving a world where there *are* things like food, tables, kids, schools, places to work, houses, yards, homes … those we love.

Am I just being a pessimist? An alarmist? A paranoid?

That's what they said about those folks who back before 1914 who were trying to get people to pay attention — over 17,000,000 people then died in the conflagration of World War I.

That's what they said about many alarmed but certainly better informed folks in the 1920s and 1930s, who said that the Treaty of Versailles was a prescription for major disaster and could only end in a catastrophic conflict. 72,000,000 dead bodies from the greatest war in human history — so far — proved them right.

History repeats itself again and again … until it doesn't.

Until there is no more history.

Until it's all gone, and there is no longer anyone left to be annoyed by pleas for sanity and prayers for peace.

Then the planet will be governed by a vast, all-embracing quiet, when only the scurrying of cockroaches across a dusty, barren landscape offers evidence of life on Earth.

Obama's Neocons and Other Hawkish Lunatics

People often don't see the obvious.

I constantly get criticized for maintaining that Obama is a warmonger. The president's actions are proof positive: His escalating of the war in Afghanistan, his engineering the destruction of Libya, his manufacturing the crisis in Ukraine, his demonizing Putin and resurrecting the Cold War with Russia, his infamous kill lists and callous use of drones in countries like Pakistan and Yemen.

Most recently, there was his request for unlimited war powers, a new AUMF — Authorization for Use of Military Force — a shrewdly, deceptively worded legislative act which allows him to attack any country, anywhere on the earth, targeting individuals, groups and nations which he alone decides are deserving of some tough love — aka annihilation by military force.

If this weren't incriminating enough, just look at the people he is surrounded by.

First, the hard-core psychopaths …

Ashton Carter is Obama's new Secretary of Defense. He wants confrontation with Russia; advocates a "preventive war" on North Korea, i.e. blow them to kingdom come now rather than later; and thinks we need to mount an aggressive campaign to fight ISIS. I guess he finds it easy to overlook the fact that our other aggressive campaigns *created* ISIS, that they are using the armaments we introduced into the region for *their* aggressive campaign, that every aggressive campaign we have mounted in the Middle East has recruited more fanatics and  terrorists, an established fact which has been verified by our own security agencies. Carter is an unapologetic proponent of projecting America's military across the globe, without respect for the national interests of any other sovereign powers and without patience for the niceties of diplomacy.

James Clapper is Director of National Intelligence, and is by any measure Spy-Master-In-Chief. He recently distinguished himself by lying under oath to the U.S. Congress, evidence that he believes that as head of a major law enforcement agency, he himself is above the law. Like other neocon exceptionalists, he believes the U.S. itself is above the law, thus entitled to ignore treaties, international legal precedents, and anything America finds bothersome. He recently threw his flaming hat into the ring of international politics by advocating sending lethal weapons to Ukraine, violating the terms of the Minsk II agreement which has offered some hope for the end of the bloody conflict, and more destructively, antagonizing Russia, which has over the past year worked relentlessly to broker peace there. But why would Clapper want peace? That might end up reducing his bloated share of the federal budget.

Victoria Nuland is Assistant Secretary of State for European and Eurasian Affairs and married to Robert Kagan, one of the founders of the neocon Project for the New American Century. She was instrumental in turning the Maidan demonstrations into a full-blown coup, an illegal, violent overthrow of the admittedly corrupt but still democratically elected Ukraine government. She continues to sabotage any hope for a negotiated solution to the crisis she helped to orchestrate and create. She is virulently anti-Russian and militantly in favor of dismembering the country to expedite the control and plundering of Russia's abundant natural resources, as well as those of the Ukraine, for the benefit of American-backed banks and corporations.

General Philip M. Breedlove is the former Supreme Allied Commander Europe (SACEUR) of NATO Allied Command Operations. He has had a remarkable career indeed, but his recent detachment from reality and delusions of grandeur have made him the major proponent for war on Russia in the E.U. theater of command. His constant spewing of venomous anti-Russian rhetoric and wild claims have made him both a laughingstock and a thorn in the side of the saner members of the European community, who for some reason don't want Europe to become an incinerated pile of rubble in service to the American dream of world hegemony. If Russian troops and equipment had invaded Ukraine as many times as General Breedlove has claimed — against all evidence to the contrary — half of the Russian military would be set up in vast emplacements visible from the moon with a cheap pair of binoculars. But you know those cagey Russians! They made everything invisible! They're there! Really. Just ask Breedlove.

U.S. Ambassador to Ukraine, Geoffrey Pyatt is a California guy with a very shallow, checkered career in the diplomatic services, which makes him the perfect tool to go about the business of spreading propaganda, sidling up to chocolate king Petro Poroshenko — current President of Ukraine — for photo ops and general glad-handing, and promoting the depraved neocon agenda, unburdened by a comprehension of the complexities of international relations, indifferent to the human suffering being inflicted on citizens in the East of the country, and cavalier about the potential for nuclear war the machinations of the U.S. is creating. Snatching war and death from the jaws of peace and harmony? All in a days work!

Then, there are those without official neocon credentials but who embrace undisguised bullying and unrestrained militarism.

Samantha Power, U.S. Ambassador to the United Nations, seemed over the course of much of her career to have her heart in the right place. She cared so much about victims of genocide, she even wrote a Pulitzer Prize-winning book about it, *A Problem From Hell: America and the Age of Genocide*. She has stood strong for religious freedom, human rights, women's and LGBT rights, and campaigned against human trafficking and for protection of refugees and religious minorities.

Unfortunately, lately she's become very confused. She wants to accomplish these noble things by bombing everyone into submission. She was instrumental in the destruction of Libya, and now her weepy voice can be heard at the United Nations spreading propaganda and subjecting the world to her acrimonious diatribes promoting chaos and violence. Power issues shrill catcalls demonizing Putin, often rails against Russia, then without blinking prevaricates about the actual role the U.S. has played in the Ukraine. What happens to these people? Is there some mutant strain of warmongering meningitis going around?

Vice-President Joe Biden and Secretary of State John Kerry put a unique spin on an old tactic. Instead of doing the familiar GOOD COP/BAD COP routine, these veteran clowns do BAD COP/WORSE COP — each of them vying to be more obnoxious, deceptive, and counterproductive than the other.

Joe Biden has always been a straight-talker, unafraid to lay it on the line, paint stark images in bold strokes, whether he made sense or not. He shoots from the hip and often ends up with his foot in his mouth. The problem now is not his candor. It's his rancor.

That and his willingness to ignore facts and be a complete stooge for policies which at best are misguided, or at worst will plunge America and Europe into another major war. He and Kerry have already alienated Russia, undone years of diplomacy, unraveled the trust that had slowly built over decades, and launched Cold War 2.0, a frightening confrontation which has the potential to bankrupt the country, if not trigger the nuclear holocaust of World War III. Joe just can't shut up. Maybe the gaffs were funny before, but it's hard to get a giggle going when we're facing human extinction.

Unlike Biden who is a full-out puncher, the more guileful John Kerry is a master of the feint and duck. He'll often use the Rope-A-Dope to keep everyone off-balance, as if this vindicates the havoc he will in the end remorselessly inflict. His pronouncements combined with Obama's has turned a peaceful and generally promising detente with Russia into a hostile and dangerous game of chicken. Along the way, Kerry has managed to alienate many of America's most trusted allies, and create panic and hysteria among many former nations of the Soviet bloc. When not hiding behind his adorable impersonation of Pepe Le Pew, he's threatening, intimidating, bullying, and overall a bombastic buffoon.

Ladies and gentlemen: We need to take stock.

If these lunatics are allowed to continue, they will not rest until they destroy the world.

These folks are so blind, so arrogant, so incapable of perspective and moral sensibility, so drunk on power and possessed by delusions of imperial grandeur and world conquest, so out of touch and incapable of common sense and common decency, so lacking empathy and basic kindness, they are happy risking nuclear annihilation to see their misguided priorities and psychopathic visions prevail.

Obama's foreign policy is a box of chocolates. Except you *always* know what you're going to get — more war, more bombing, more drone assassinations, more innocent civilian deaths, more illegal regime change, more chaos and destruction.

Then again, what else can we expect? It's the company he keeps. Obama is surrounded by bloodthirsty, arguably mad, imperialist warmongers, megalomaniacs who see themselves as saviors of the Universe, chosen by destiny and blessed with infallibility. Were any of them to undergo sound and objective psychological testing, they would immediately be committed to maximum-security institutions for the criminally insane.

However, America treats them differently.

It elevates them to the highest positions of power.

More Bases More Bombs More War

U.S. Military Troops and Bases Around the World

"The United States military is currently deployed to more locations than it has been throughout history."

—Dept. of Defense.

Sources: Dept. of Defense, "Base Structure Report, FY 2002" and "Active Duty Military Personnel Strengths by Regional area and by Country, Dec. 31, 2001"; Zoltan Grossman, "New U.S. Military Bases." Feb. 2, 2002; Monthly Review, 2002

☐ 45 countries with no U.S. military presence
☐ 156 countries with U.S. troops
☐ 63 countries with U.S. military bases and troops
☐ 7 countries with 13 new U.S. military bases since 9/11/2001
In 2001, the U.S. had 255,065 troops abroad

They say things have to get worse before they get better.

But how much worse can the U.S. and the world tolerate?

Driven purely by institutional self-preservation and relentless pursuit of profits by the military-industrial-complex, the cancer of American military presence continues to metastasize unchecked across the planet. Not satisfied with creating tens of thousands of new terrorists since 9/11 with aggressive wars, invasions, special ops initiatives, drone bombing, assassinations — all in all claiming the lives of over a million innocent civilians — budgetary allocations are in place and plans being implemented for even more bases in Asia, Africa, Europe, even the Arctic.

Is it any surprise that when America sets up a new military hub in a foreign country, conflict and war soon follow?

It's a closed feedback loop where a cure sets up the conditions for the disease it's supposed to treat. If an area is relatively at peace, the putative guarantees of continuing tranquility offered by our military presence will produce opposition and rivalry which inevitably will metastasize into conflict and war.

On that note, there certainly is no mystery why terrorism is on the rise, especially in Middle Eastern countries.

Osama bin Laden stated it clearly. To paraphrase …

"We don't want you here!"

Not only is sovereignty at issue in these native lands, but often they host sites which are considered sacred in both social and political traditions which stretch back centuries. The very presence of U.S. soldiers, war planes, drones, or any of the other paraphernalia of empire is insult enough. But the slaughter of innocent individuals, too often women and children, can only evoke cries of outrage and demands for revenge. Is it asking too much to imagine how U.S. citizens would react if a wedding party was blown to bits in Topeka, Kansas or Knoxville, Tennessee?

This must end. The unnecessary expansion of U.S. military presence throughout the world is bankrupting our economy, incriminating each and every American citizen in horrifying war crimes, and risking World War III. Ultimately it will collapse the nation and take down the great American experiment.

It's up to us to stop this before it's too late!

The *Peace Dividend* is where we start.

"I hate war!"

"I hate war!"

Of course, you do!

Most of us hate seeing mutilated corpses, burning buildings, destroyed villages and towns, starving homeless refugees.

Yet, America has been at war for 223 years of its 240 year history!

How is this possible?

If we all hate war so much, why are we constantly at war?

Why … ?

Peace?

Has America ever really had a peace movement?

Yes, there was an anti-war movement in the late 60s, early 70s.

But it was an *anti-war* movement … specific to one particular war.

The Vietnam War.

Why?

Because young people — I was the perfect age and in the thick of it — didn't want to get blown away in some rice paddy in a country in Asia they could barely find on a map.

It was survival.

Demonstrate.

Burn your draft cards.

Stay alive!

To be for peace *in principle* means you are values-driven.

But Americans for the most part are results-driven.

Get the job done. Get the job done right. Miller time.

Which troublingly is a short leap to "the ends justify the means".

To see how that works out, just ask the survivors of Dresden, Hiroshima, Nagasaki.

Ask the citizens of Iraq, Afghanistan, Libya, Haiti, Honduras, Nicaragua, Kosovo, Yemen.

Get the job done. Get it done right. Watch the Super Bowl.

Peace is a warm and fuzzy idea. It's something you can wriggle right up to, get all friendly, pinch its cute little cheeks, coddle it like a newborn, smile for the camera.

Yes, peace is really awesome!

As long as you don't have to be <u>peaceful</u>.

Therein lies the conundrum.

America likes to kick ass! It's our way or the highway.

It's our way or you better head for a bomb shelter, *mofo!*

America is tough. You know where America stands.

America wears its temperament on its sleeve.

It open-carries its guns … fair warning.

Don't even think about it!

Mess with me and you're dead meat!

Doesn't exactly sound like fertile ground for a peace movement, eh?

However, peace signs are great!

Simple and attractive.

Makes a great tattoo.

Charm bracelet. Bumper sticker.

They're compact, symmetrical.

Blend in nicely anywhere.

OH YEAH! PEACE, BROTHER!

It's a MAD MAD World

Appropriately named MAD — Mutual Assured Destruction — it has been in place since the 1950s and constitutes a strategy of deterrence whereby both Russia and the U.S. refrains from using their vast nuclear arsenals because both know their nations and probably the rest of the world would be destroyed. This bilateral suicide pact has been keeping the world "safe" for over half a century.

Now the U.S. in its quest for ultimate superiority and global supremacy is chipping away at it, installing ABM systems on Russia's borders, literally *creating* a powerful incentive for them to "get this over with". It literally makes it a rational choice for each side to get a jump on the other and by initiating a pre-emptive strike.

I don't think Russia will hit the launch buttons. Despite all of the venomous anti-Russian propaganda and Putin-bashing going on right now in the U.S., Russia has been militarily a defensive nation for several hundred years. This is also true of China. Especially compared to the U.S. and its allies, both Russia and China have been notably *unaggressive* in their pursuit of power and standing in the world.

That's not to say either nation will cower before the chest-thumping of America's relentless pursuit of military superiority and world domination.

Without any doubt, given what both countries have suffered historically at the hands of aggressors both in the Asia and the Europe theaters of war, one can be absolutely certain they will stand their ground.

Yet, building on its almost perfect record of losing every conflict it has either started or been involved with since WWII, the U.S. is creating the conditions for confrontation with China with its "pivot to Asia", and pushing all the wrong buttons by starting the conflict in Ukraine, then prompting a number of countries on Russia's borders to station missiles and augment their military against an imagined threat of Russian aggression.

I'm not going to not pull punches here. Obama, Biden, Kerry, Clinton before him, and the entire rat pack of power-crazed imperialists are driving the America and the world toward war — the war to end all wars, because it *will* indeed end everything.

Hasn't the world had enough conflict, destruction and carnage?

Do any of these people read history?

Is there any way to explain all of the self-sabotaging maneuvering going on right now?

Let's look at this with the clarity and objectivity you and I and most Americans have by virtue of living outside the Washington DC bubble, away from the imperious fantasy world of our neocon-infested government.

Who in their right mind would come up with MAD, then destabilize it with policies which replace its precarious, paranoid, hair-trigger brinkmanship with more confrontation and a renewed arms race?

Aah . . . maybe I'm on to something!

Who in their *right mind* . . .?

Look at this inventory of nuclear weapons:

Country	Deployed warheads	Other warheads	Total inventory
USA	~2 080	5 180	~7 260
Russia	~1 780	~5 720	~7 500
UK	150	~65	~215
France	~290	~10	~300
China	–	~260	~260
India	–	90–110	90–110
Pakistan	–	100–120	100–120
Israel	–	~80	~80
North Korea	..	..	6–8
Total	**~4 300**	**~11 545**	**~15 850**

sipri   All figures are approximate and are as of January 2015.

www.sipri.org

Does this compute?

There are something like 15,850 nuclear bombs in the world?

Most of them are hundreds of times as destructive as the only two atomic weapons ever used, the ones dropped on Hiroshima and Nagasaki by the U.S. at the very end of World War II. Those two comparatively tiny nuclear weapons instantly killed over 100,000 people. Many more subsequently died from burns and radiation sickness.

Who in their *right mind . . .*?

This Is War

1992 © KENNETH JARECKE (CONTACT PRESS IMAGES)

Until recently, this photo was never seen in the U.S. It's a soldier making a last desperate attempt at climbing out of a military vehicle after it had been hit by an incendiary bomb. This was during Desert Storm in 1991.

This is the side of war our leaders don't want you to see. For us they want it to be all about waving flags, marching bands, grandiose speeches, stars-and-stripes lapel pins.

Remember George W's order that there be no reporting of coffins flown in from Afghanistan and Iraq containing the remains of our dead soldiers?

But this photo is what war is really all about. That scorched corpse could be your son or daughter, one of your grandchildren, an uncle, cousin, nephew or niece, that freckled neighborhood kid that used to ride by on a bike.

When our politicians speak about some new crisis that requires our military intervention, some challenge to our national interests or terrorist threat to the homeland, then with the appropriate somber expressions and deeply-furrowed brows reel off patriotic slogans and chest-thumping battle cries that beg for our bravado and self-sacrifice, they want you to imagine proud soldiers in clean pressed uniforms, glorious fireworks reflecting in the pool of the national mall, the flag majestically waving in the background atop the White House. They want you embracing that triumphant feeling of being a citizen of the greatest country in the world. They most certainly do not want you thinking about that photograph.

Sure, our leaders claim that they want to avoid at all costs sending our brave soldiers into harms way. They claim to value every young man and woman in uniform as they do their own children — though for some reason their own kids never get sent into battle.

They claim the decision to wage war, even to commit our troops to "limited engagement", is a very serious one, that putting "boots on the ground" is something we do only when every other conceivable option has been duly explored, considered, weighed, exhausted.

Warning! When you hear any of this talk about war as a last resort, be VERY AFRAID. Because it means the bombs are about to drop and the bullets are about to fly. Last resort is now pure cover, a charade, just one component of a PR game to tenderize public opinion, just more cynical role play to get people ready for the slaughter.

When our leaders say they hate war, be VERY ANGRY. Because their actions betray their love — their worship! — of military power. Just look at their priorities. Just look at the national budget. Just take out a world map and try to identify the 900+ military bases the U.S. has in over 145 countries across the globe. If they really wanted peace, these would be Peace Corps camps, not military installations.

When they talk about "humanitarian war" and "R2P" — responsibility to protect — LAUGH, then CRY. Because any humanitarian concern is not about you. And when you're getting your ass shot at, the only reason they want to protect you is so you can shoot back.

On the increasingly rare occasions, when our leaders do give their token nod to promoting peace in the world, be INDIGNANT — be OUTRAGED — at the blatant hypocrisy. Why, our Nobel Peace Prize winning president even used his award acceptance speech to make the case for "necessary wars".

Let's see ... necessary wars. When I was in college, it was Vietnam. Commies would take over the world if we didn't stop them. Then we had to stop Saddam Hussein from taking over Kuwait, even though 9 out of 10 American thought Kuwait was a tropical fruit. Then, of course, we had to bomb the shit out of Afghanistan to catch Osama bin Laden, though he strutted around the caves and continued to make threatening videos for the next eight years. Then, we *really* had to get Saddam Hussein, this time before he dropped an atomic bomb on Baltimore or Orlando, even if he didn't have one and if he did had no way to lob it further than the Sea of Galilee. Then there was Libya because we had to get rid of that pesky Gaddafi. And Syria because ... well, just because. And of course, we've been having a regular hissy fit about Iran for decades now, so they're high on the hit list. And now we have the Ukraine, for a lot of reasons, including Snowden, and Putin's making Obama look like a warmonger, which frankly is not that hard, and the BRICS, and the abandonment of the dollar, and the deranged neocons running amok in the State Department, and the piles of military hardware which we're bankrupting the country to buy — after all, you can't just leave that stuff laying around, because it's dangerous, so it's *imperative* we use it. Hell, let's throw some ordnance at the Russkies, and the Chinese ... and ... and ...

Whew! All these "necessary wars" are exhausting!

As anyone who reads my books knows, I rarely recommend any organization or direct readers to support its activities. There are hundreds — thousands — of good, hard-working, well-meaning, probably extremely worthwhile groups out there trying to make a difference. My reluctance stems from observing that despite their best efforts, not a lot seems to be getting done.

But now, since time is running out and this might be our last best hope, I'm going to break tradition.

Please go to the website for World Beyond War ...

http://www.worldbeyondwar.org/

One of the founding members and its current director is a man I greatly respect and admire, David Swanson. There is a wealth of information on the web site itself but here is a quick summary of their agenda:

- Creating an easily recognizable and joinable mainstream international movement to end all war.
- Education about war, peace, and nonviolent action — including all that is to be gained by ending war.
- Improving access to accurate information about wars. Exposing falsehoods.
- Improving access to information about successful steps away from war in other parts of the world.
- Increased understanding of partial steps as movement in the direction of eliminating, not reforming, war.
- Partial and full disarmament.
- Conversion or transition to peaceful industries.
- Closing, converting or donating foreign military bases.

- Democratizing militaries while they exist and making them truly volunteer.
- Banning foreign weapons sales and gifts.
- Outlawing profiteering from war.
- Banning the use of mercenaries and private contractors.
- Abolishing the CIA and other secret agencies.
- Promoting diplomacy and international law, and consistent enforcement of laws against war, including prosecution of violators.
- Reforming or replacing the U.N. and the ICC.
- Expansion of peace teams and human shields.
- Promotion of nonmilitary foreign aid and crisis prevention.
- Placing restrictions on military recruitment and providing potential soldiers with alternatives.
- Thanking resisters for their service.
- Encouraging cultural exchange.
- Discouraging racism and nationalism.
- Developing less destructive and exploitative lifestyles.
- Expanding the use of public demonstrations and nonviolent civil resistance to enact all of these changes.

Is it naive to think that the human race can rise above its long history of savagery?

In a thought-provoking article at The Huffington Post, titled "How Many Minutes to Midnight?", Noam Chomsky says we are a "strange species which attained the intelligence to discover the effective means to destroy itself, but — so the evidence suggests — not the moral and intellectual capacity to control its worst instincts."

Let's hope he's wrong.

Part III

Peace Dividend: The U.S. Public Takes Control of Its Destiny

War Is A Lie

We all know what's going on in Syria. There's been a civil war for some time now. Many citizens there are very unhappy with the Assad regime. There are elements within the country, now joined by a variety of well-armed and well-funded terrorist organizations from outside, that have taken up arms in an attempt to overthrow the government.

We also know that Washington DC — I obviously include here Obama, Biden, Hillary Clinton before and now Kerry, but also the huge embedded coterie of neocon imperialists who never look at a military campaign they don't get all giddy over and have grandiose visions of American hegemony over the world that goes way beyond childish fantasy into the realm of delusional psychosis — has been licking its lips for a long time now, waiting for the right moment and the most plausible opportunity to plunge our country into another pointless military conflict in the Middle East. Iran's alleged development of a nuclear weapon just hasn't gotten traction so far with the American public — basically because it's a fabrication. Hmm ... what else might get everyone's hackles up?

We have heard claims of "irrefutable proof" that chemical weapons were used by Assad's forces against Syria's own people. We hear the "irrefutable logic" that this gross violation of proscriptions against use of such weapons — international law in the form of treaties and legal instruments by the United Nations — MUST be punished. We've heard that Assad drops bottle bombs, whatever they are, on innocent civilians because he's a sadistic, brutal tyrant who apparently gets off on blowing people up.

The need to provide actual evidence for any of this never comes up.

To their credit, most Americans are not buying the thunderous but hollow beating of the war drums. Tragically the express will of the citizenry is not deterring the warmongers. These guys are relentless. They'll keep pouring it on. They'll come up with whatever "facts and figures" — just make them up if necessary — it takes to turn the tide of opinion and convince us to get with the program.

But the simple truth is . . . it's all a lie.

Either it's a lie via the lack of certain evidence.

Or it's a lie which springs from America's own hypocrisy.

America MUST punish such immoral transgressions?

First of all, there are mechanisms in place for addressing any such violations. America is not required to be judge, jury and executioner here or in any other instance of misbehavior by other nations. It adopts this role out of convenience, when it supports some hidden agenda which is kept from the public. Informed, independent political analysts know, for example, that the ongoing project of regime change in Syria is about 1) oil and gas pipelines, and 2) destroying opposition to Israel in the region.

Second, our indignation at the atrocities committed in other countries rings very hollow when you consider how America tends to cherry-pick its moral outrage. For example, we looked the other way when Saddam Hussein was gassing Iran. You remember. Saddam Hussein, that evil bad guy we had to depose. The one we tagged as the new Hitler. The one we supported with billions of dollars of foreign aid a few years before when we liked him, the despicable evil dictator of the country where we "initiated and supported much of the financing, intelligence, and military help that built Saddam's Iraq into the power it became" and "Reagan/Bush administrations permitted — and frequently encouraged — the flow of money, agricultural credits, dual-use technology, chemicals, and weapons to Iraq."

I won't even get into the list of countries where we stood by and yawned, as the slaughter of tens of thousands of innocent people occurred — Rwanda immediately comes to mind — our indignation on holiday. Nor will I get into the incredibly long list of countries ruled by ruthless autocrats supported by the U.S., who oppress and slaughter their own people often with the armaments we provide them.

While I'm on the subject of lies, I'm sure I don't have to remind you of all of the lies — WMDs being first on the list — told to the American people and the entire world which plunged us into the Iraq war, at the cost of 5,000 American lives and 190,000 Iraqis, 70% of them citizens. And how to make the medicine go down nice and smooth, we were told prior to that horrible fiasco, that we should be able to get in, get out, and wrap up the military campaign for a mere $50 or $60 billion, whereas estimates for the financial burdens *just from the Iraq war* are now at $2.2 trillion (yes, that's TRILLION!).

So ...

Why all these lies?

Obviously, lies serve a specific timely function in terms of swaying public opinion. For example, whenever we're getting ready to put boots on the ground, we have to get people riled up before we send our young men and women into combat. Or even before wasting billions of our tax dollars raining down death and destruction on another country in the form of cruise missiles. Otherwise, some armchair generals might come to the conclusion that these wars are nothing more than senseless slaughter. Even if they are purely senseless slaughter, we can't have people *thinking that!*

But even beyond the practical needs of our amoral, trigger-happy, ends-justify-the-means political leaders, I see something happening in our society. It's certainly nothing new, but what is unprecedented is its scale.

I've come to believe that lying has become pandemic. Not only is it acceptable. It's become woven into the fabric of our culture, the way cancer cells weave their way into the anatomy of the human body.

Why do *THEY* lie and tell young girls they're not pretty enough, not thin enough, not sexy enough, and then lie to them about cosmetics, diets and weight loss pills, fashions that will turn them into objects of allure?

Why do *THEY* lie to young men and tell them might makes right and if you have a big gun or big muscles or a big mouth or a big dick, you now own the high moral ground and you can bully your way and everyone will think you're a stud or a hero?

Why do *THEY* lie to all of us regular folks and still call America the land of opportunity, where no matter how poor you are or what color your skin, you can rise to the top, when the truth is *upward mobility in the U.S. is the worst in the developed world?*

Why?

Why all the lies?

Amazingly enough, there is one answer.

One size fits all.

These mega liars keep it simple.

Money!

Behind every lie we're told is a profit motive. Every lie that succeeds takes money from you and I and puts it into the pockets of the liars.

I know this sounds simplistic. But the truth is the already appallingly wealthy just can't get enough. Already in possession of the vast majority of this country's wealth, they want more. They want it all.

What's Syria about? The full explanation would take up an hour of your time. But as I already pointed out, it's about pipelines — gas and oil pipelines.

That's what Afghanistan was about. That's what Iraq was about. That's what Iran is about. That's what Syria is about. If you have the time and have a strong stomach — it certainly made me sick — watch these videos to see why our soldiers are dying:

"Syria, what is really going on and why" YouTube
https://www.youtube.com/watch?v=L4vD6JpJAFI

"It's all about the PIPELINE. Syria, Iran, Arab Spring, etc." YouTube
http://www.youtube.com/watch?v=Rw5Z3OxdCxc

"Pepe Escobar, Paraguay, Syria, Pipelines, oh my." YouTube
https://www.youtube.com/watch?v=artcLfC9t_A

Wars are always built on lies. I am totally convinced of this now. Syria is just the latest example in a very long, disturbing list.

Let me also recommend you buy David Swanson's book (pictured at the head of this section) ... http://davidswanson.org/warisalie.

He doesn't know me and I get no commission. I have no stake in this.

But you do. If you don't read this book, you're choosing a lobotomy over understanding why we are immersed in gridlock, confusion, conundrum. Why we're perpetually at war. Why we, who have to go out and put our lives on the line for the rich and powerful, are always given this choice:

a) War
b) War
c) All of the above

Does this sound twisted or melodramatic? It's not.

When you see the reason behind all the lies, it's like when Dorothy arrived in Oz and suddenly her world went from black-and-white to dazzling, breathtaking color.

Let me say one last thing about lies and war. This applies to every waking moment of our lives, and why we must always be vigilantes for honesty.

When *THEY* lie to us and we believe them, we end up at war with ourselves, war with one another, war with everyone else in the world, and at war with the truth.

And if we continue to allow this to happen ...

There will be no survivors.

Give Peace A Chance

Before the jingoistic cheer leading, Russia-hating catcalls, and venomous Putin insults start pouring from the poorly informed but enthusiastically irrational peanut gallery, let's take a moment to review a few important FACTS. Maybe FACTS are not quite as spectacular or emotionally satisfying as burping up bilious gas balls of MSM propaganda, but they can provide PERSPECTIVE.

During the 90s, following the dissolution of the USSR, the military flights and air-space patrols and probing by Russia as part of their stand-off with the West — mirrored 24/7 by the U.S. and NATO with similar fleets of fighters, bombers, reconnaissance planes, refueling tankers — stopped completely. The reconnaissance and war readiness exercises by the Western powers, however, continued uninterrupted.

Reacting to this unbroken protraction of war readiness by the West, Russia started up their long range bomber patrols again July and August 2007, returned to guarding its air space and borders, keeping a sufficient number of planes in the air to let the West know that they were not to be permitted carte blanche superiority in the skies near Russian air space.

This means, for over 15 years Russia suspended a major component of the Cold War years confrontation, taking itself completely off of a war footing. Rather than take advantage of this historic opportunity, the West continued, and if anything increased, its intimidation of Russia, which by both choice and circumstance — its empire had disintegrated and the country itself was in dire economic straits — tried to pursue peaceful relations.

During the 90s Russia was understandably preoccupied with putting its house back in order and trying to rebuild the functional framework of a nation. With calculating deftness but in direct violation of recorded assurances made to Russia that NATO would not move "one inch east" of Germany — a trade-off for Russia's quickly withdrawing its troops from East Germany to permit an orderly, uncontested reunification of the German nation — NATO at the prompting of the U.S. proceeded to rapidly expand its geographical orbit. Today it includes Poland, Hungary, Czech Republic, Croatia, Latvia, Lithuania, Estonia, Slovakia, Romania, Bulgaria, and Slovenia. All of these countries are considerably more than an inch east of Germany.

Then in December 2001, the U.S. announced that it was unilaterally pulling out of the ABM Treaty, signaling that it claimed the right to now put anti-ballistic missiles in any country in the NATO alliance. This move was unprovoked, meaning there was no specific incident or level of tension between Russia and the U.S. prompting such a sudden and dramatic breach of the agreement, one that had been in force since 1972. Ominously, this was the first time in U.S. history that America had walked away from such a major agreement.

Since the U.S. at the time and for many years afterwards, claimed that the anti-ballistic missiles were purely to prevent rogue nations like Iran and North Korea from attacking Europe, Russia offered to become part of a unified system of missile defense of Europe, proffering its own sophisticated missile tracking radar to the mix.

America *turned down* this offer from the Russians.

While there is much more, sometimes less is more.

Here less is enough.

Encapsulating ...

NATO moves its military alliance and bases to Russia's borders. The U.S. starts deploying ABMs near Russia's borders. The U.S. wants no part of Russian cooperation in optimizing those systems against the "enemies".

Who is Russia to conclude is the *real enemy* being targeted by these ABMs?

What is Russia to conclude from the relentless move east, right up to its borders, of the military forces of NATO?

What is Russia to conclude from what appears to be a "containment" policy directed at them, currently implemented by twenty-seven major military installations, with possibly more yet to come?

Then to pour gasoline on the embers of suspicion, last year the U.S. assisted the overthrow of a democratically elected government in Ukraine, a nation with *long* historical ties going back centuries to Russia, located right on Russia's "underbelly".

Concurrently, a venomous anti-Russia propaganda blitz began in the West. Everything became Russia's fault: The whole Ukraine crisis, the downing of Malaysian Flight 17, the deaths in eastern Ukraine, the "invasion" and annexation of Crimea. No evidence was forthcoming. Just accusations.

About the same time, a massive campaign to demonize Putin went into high gear, initiated and aggressively promoted by the U.S. via its presstitute media — direct personal attacks even made by Obama, Biden, and Samantha Power at the U.N. — and spread across the globe, the truculence championed by England, Germany and France.

What is going on here? What does this look like to *you*?

I know what it looks like to *me*. There is not a shred of doubt in my mind that hubris and arrogance, that delusional imperial ambitions and diplomatic megalomania, coupled with just plain horrible judgment has again replaced thoughtful analysis, basic respect for the interests of other nations, and responsible leadership.

Many are coming to this horrifying conclusion: America *wants* war with Russia.

It doesn't help that some clueless imbeciles escaped their short bus ride for a day at the Leggo Park and infiltrated our policy-making institutions, preaching the suicidal gospel that we can *win* a nuclear war with Russia. They are joined by self-proclaimed political geniuses — masters of the universe who think history is a 90s Michael Jackson album — proposing after consulting their Magic 8-Ball that with a few slick moves America can just topple the current government of Russia and render the entire nation with its vast natural resources a vassal state, ready for easy picking by America's corporate predators. I'm sure these same Pollyannas also believe that the

Russian people will welcome America, weeping for joy, throwing bouquets before our Humvees as they roll through Moscow Square.

America *thinks* it can bluster and bluff, use color revolutions to nudge Putin out of office and install some bloated puppet in his place like they did with Poroshenko in Ukraine — though even that's far from a done deal itself.

America *thinks* what it says is divine truth and to hell with anyone who disagrees.

America *thinks* its military might and economic power confers it a special, unassailable place in the world, a position of supreme and unquestionable leadership and iron rule.

With these recent dealings with Russia, we're another 24 years into the tragicomedy of our infantile machinations, self-absorbed exceptionalism, diplomatic myopia, and sociopathic delusions of imperial grandeur. We have engaged some of the best minds and produced some of the worst ideas.

Where do we now stand?

What do we have to show for all of this American ingenuity?

First and foremost, Cold War 2.0 is up and running full-tilt because Russia *finally* arrived at the inescapable conclusion that NATO is a profound military threat.

The meticulously and arduously fashioned trust and spirit of cooperation gradually built over decades is trashed, relations between the U.S. and Russia severely damaged for many years to come. Russia now believes all of the talk of integration and cooperation was just lip-service, a cheap smokescreen for America's real agenda — destroying their country.

As accusations and hysteria prompted by old habits and grudges now take center stage, hopeful and constructive dialogue have become drown out by the drums of war.

War fever and sabotage of peace initiatives — mostly emanating from Washington DC — are becoming pandemic.

The escalation of paranoia and preparation for major conflict keeps ratcheting up and up.

Trying to stop this madness is like trying to stop an avalanche with a pair of wool mittens.

We are way beyond the finger-pointing and blame-game phase. Now it's tit-for-tat as both sides ramp up their respective militaries, each new step bringing the situation closer to spinning completely out of control.

The Pentagon pushes for a military build-up along Russia's border. The world gets to hear General Frederick Hodges explain his no-mercy policy and lecture Europe and NATO about preparedness. Friction develops and Russia objects as NATO continues a massive military build-up of troops in the Baltic States and other Eastern Europe NATO countries. There are U.S. paratroopers headed for Ukraine to train their army. Ukraine President Petro Poroshenko, claims to have struck a deal will eleven EU countries to provide military weapons, including lethal ones. Great Britain deploys 30 Royal Air Force planes for Rising Panther, its largest war aerial exercises in a decade, in response to the "Russian threat". U.S. tanks, Humvees and armored personnel carriers roll through Latvia. We have JOINT WARRIOR, a huge deployment of naval ships out of Scotland, for war game exercises. Poland is purchasing the Patriot ABM system to defend against the anticipated Russian invasion. Even the U.S. National Guard has sent twelve F-15 interceptor jets to Europe guarding against Russia.

None of this has escaped Russia's attention, so understandably they have responded with their own build-up and heightened alert status. They conducted huge rapid deployment drills in Kaliningrad, and have deployed a new missile defense radar system there which covers the entire Atlantic. Russia is sending advanced supersonic strategic bombers to Crimea for global training exercises, as well as re-equipping early warning radar sites in the recently annexed territory. They have also announced the launch of a new advanced missile-attack warning satellite. There have been reports of an escalating presence of Russian strategic bombers near U.S. airspace, and concern expressed by NATO at the apparently growing number of "incidents" involving Russian planes and seagoing vessels, with of course no mention of the provocations emanating from NATO itself and its allies. Recognizing that Russia will stand toe-to-toe with the West in the face of aggression by NATO, U.S. troops at the front now feel "vulnerable" and want bigger, better weapons.

Through all of this, a stream of propaganda, outright condemnation, shoddy fabrication, angry provocation, and malicious innuendo continue to spew from President Obama, Vice-President Biden, Secretary of State Kerry, and U.S. Ambassador to the United Nations, Samantha Power, aided and abetted naturally by the main stream media.

To cap off this inventory of disastrous developments, we have the likes of Geoffrey Pyatt — a man with a long sleazy record of diplomatic disservice — who is currently U.S. Ambassador to the Ukraine, apparently tweeting an image of Russian air defense systems, claiming they were there in the country, when in fact the photo was actually taken outside of Moscow two years prior at an International Aviation and Space Show. Mr. Pyatt has thus expanded the range of his incompetence to even being pathetic at lying — making him more dangerous.

Alarmingly, we now have the perfect storm: hubris, idiocy, and paranoia. The military one upmanship coupled with diplomatic dysfunction is sheer madness.

I keep listening for a voice of sanity, encouraging appeals for restraint, some thoughtful analysis — occasionally there have been a few faint whispers — but mostly I'm hearing adolescent boys shouting at one another, as they rev up for a serious scrap in the schoolyard.

At the same time, as with most fights someone had to start it. Usually that gives us some clue who needs to stop it.

No matter what spin you put on everything I've laid out in this section, no matter how you rationalize it, hide it behind the thin vapor of noble intentions, tuck it into self-righteous teleprompter sound bites, and massage it with increasingly hollow-sounding justifications, without any equivocation, doubt, or splitting of hairs, it is the *U.S. that has been provoking and perpetuating* this *extremely dangerous* and *patently counter-productive* confrontation.

It's not in America's long term interests to keep this war of nerves going.

The longer it goes on, the more ridiculous and desperate America appears.

Russia is not Zimbabwe, Iraq, or Yemen. It's not Grenada or Haiti.

Russia is not going to be intimidated by a chest-thumping schoolyard bully.

This can only end badly for the U.S., its allies, and the rest of the world.

Obama, Kerry, Biden, Clinton, Carter … COME ON! … *man up a little!*

Admit your mistakes. Show some self-respect. Let's see *real* leadership.

Stand up to the neocon crazies and psychopathic empire builders.

Thoughtful judgment and common sense go a long way.

Drop the arrogant posturing and cut your losses.

History will judge you more kindly.

Give peace a chance.

Starving the Beast

How do we stop it?

First … understand that the Peace Dividend refund is not a money grab. It's not some cheap stunt. You've seen the documentation we've presented in this book.

Refunding the tax dollars deceptively and fraudulently taken — stolen! — from the American public over the past 24 years is by every measure of decency, fairness, and justice, the right thing to do. It is the responsibility and duty of the U.S. government and all who are in any way involved to redress this legitimate grievance and claim by the citizens of this country.

Every single dollar returned is a step toward a reconciliation.

Every single dollar returned is fair and just compensation for the abuse the American public has endured through the 24 years of the military scam.

Every single dollar returned is money which belonged and still belongs to the American public. *It's our money!*

Every single dollar returned will be put to good and proper use, a sharp contrast to the way it has been wasted through faulty thinking, bad accounting, misdirected priorities, and sheer fraud.

Having said that, let me offer a hugely important benefit which will also accrue as a result of the Peace Dividend refund.

Every single dollar of the $4.82 trillion refunded to U.S. citizens is money the warmongers in the U.S. government WILL NOT HAVE to promote more fraudulent wars and buy more unnecessary military junk.

To put it bluntly, the DOD and the defense contractors are going to feel the pinch. *A big pinch!*

Maybe someone might be tempted to feel bad for them. But the party's over! They've had a good ride. Now it's time to put all that energy and genius to work on other things which we, the American public, believe are more important than bombs and bullets, fighter planes and submarines, missiles and nukes, killing and destroying.

The *Peace Dividend* is how we do it.

We starve the beast!

Actually, 'starve' is too strong of a word.

We'll put the beast on a strict diet. A very strict diet!

Yes, we need to defend our country. There are some bad people out there. And who knows, maybe we'll be attacked by a bunch of aliens from another solar system. We must at all times be prudent and prepared.

But the point is, we have to be reasonable as well. Using the American taxpayer as a limitless ATM machine for anything and everything the military can dream up or the maniacal fantasies the imperial lunatics bent on world conquest might want handy as the U.S. smashes every country in its path, is *not reasonable!* It's not even prudent.

In fact it's insane.

By staking our claim on this sizable sum of money — the $4.82 trillion the *Peace Dividend* requires be refunded to the American citizens — we are forcing some necessary belt-tightening. Priorities will have to be reassessed. Budgets will have to be cut. The DOD will have to learn to get the job done right, on a sensible but considerably more modest budget.

We can keep America safe without throwing mountains of money at the challenge.

In fact, as we have shown, throwing mountains of money at the problem has made both the U.S. and the rest of the world *less safe!*

Time to shift gears, change direction.

Once the beast is again lean and mean, we'll have a better perspective on what needs to be done and how to do it.

Paying It Forward

The damage is done! What good will getting our $4.82 trillion back?

We've already pointed out that putting this money back into the hands of the public — $14,952 for each and every U.S. citizen — will do phenomenal things for our economy. The U.S. economy is driven by consumer spending. Whether it's buying some new clothes for the kids, doing needed repairs on the house, taking the vacation that's been postponed for year after year, even putting a few dollars in that savings account towards future college tuition, it will all eventually come back around to produce more jobs, and subsequently more healthy spending, all without putting anyone in any further debt.

But the real value comes from the very different future embracing peace will ensure. The real value comes from escaping the stuporous mentality of manufactured crisis that's spawned a false state of siege and the constant paranoia of perpetual war.

Not being under the constant cloud of war, not living in continuous fear, knowing that neither our or our neighbor's children will be sent off to fight in some senseless war, opens possibilities and opportunities which now seem far-fetched and unrealistic.

Remember ...

The *Peace Dividend* is not a drain on our national treasury or resources. Quite to the contrary, it is an investment in our future.

It's taking tax dollars which were arrogated for erroneous and destructive purposes, then repurposing all that money toward a future that is positive and constructive for all of us, thus making a long overdue correction in our nation's path and aspirations.

Moreover ...

The *Peace Dividend* is not retribution or revenge.

It is merely reclaiming and recovering what as citizens is rightfully ours, and paying it forward to shape the kind of world we want for ourselves, our children and our children's children.

The Birthright of Every American Citizen

This is your country.

It says so right in the Constitution.

As a citizen of our representative democracy, when you are born you are immutably bestowed a say in formulating the policies and laws of the nation.

You are unequivocally handed the power to shape the kind of society which unfolds within the national borders of the United States of America.

No citizen, official, agency or organization public or private, can question, challenge, or compromise that birthright. Certainly no one can legally attempt to take it away.

Similarly, as an American citizen, you have every right to share in this nation's human and natural resources. This is not a privilege reserved only for the wealthy. Likewise with your tax dollars. The money you pay in taxes is both a maintenance fee to keep America running smoothly, and an investment in all of its endeavors. Your birthright as an American citizen means you can expect a well and properly run country, and a fair and reasonable return on your investment. Meaning that the positive good and financial rewards which accrue as a result of everything your tax dollars produces should benefit you and all other citizens, not just a privileged few who have the right connections with the people we elect to office or who are situated high in the ranks of the business and banking communities.

Sadly, greed and lust for power have put your birthright under attack.

Our country has been hijacked. Now the corporate rulers intend to do what pleases them and their pocketbooks. They have accomplished this "coup d'etat in slow motion" by wresting control of the government from the people. As per our Constitution, the shaping of the legislative framework of America is supposed to be in the hands of everyday citizens, like you and I.

But recent studies suggest that not only is democracy threatened now, it is breathing its last faint gasps, and is practically dead.

When so much power is concentrated in so few hands, the whole premise of our great nation is negated.

It's impact is profound and devastating.

You as a citizen, your voice, even your vote, becomes irrelevant.

You become a spectator, an outsider looking in as others shape the conditions under which you must live, work, raise a family.

We can fight this.

But it will require determination, focus, and discipline.

You can change things.

It's up to each and every one of us to get America back on track.

No more rule by the rich and powerful.

No more crony capitalism and democracy in name only.

If we stick together and stand strong, we can do this.

We'll take back our country one vote at a time.

We'll make our elected officials answer to us.

We'll start by demanding retribution and compensation for the deceptions and the subsequent misuse of our tax dollars.

This simple, straightforward demand is powerful.

It gains its power from its legitimacy and the simple justice it seeks.

It is a slap in the face of the arrogant and elitist .1% who have perpetrated this farce and fraud.

It's a call to action for everyday citizens to demand fairness, transparency, justice, accepting responsibility, conceding mistakes, redressing catastrophic blundering, compensating the victims — the vast majority of everyday citizens like *us* — of misguided and self-serving policies, overall doing whatever it takes to remedy the havoc and suffering caused by the "war is the only way" mentality of our national leaders and their wealthy patrons.

This is the beauty of the *Peace Dividend* strategy. In one bold stroke it wrestles back a big chunk of power from the plutocracy. If we can win on this one initiative, it will strike a decisive blow to the heart of autocratic monopoly of government by the corporate elite. It is a watershed assault on the status quo which can initiate an entire spectrum of dramatic reforms on many fronts: tax policy, foreign policy, militarization of our society, currency creation and monetary policy, electoral procedures and abuses, wealth inequality.

Most dramatically, it will demonstrate that the power of the people, the right of self-determination by everyday citizens, is still viable.

Plus ...

America will again be viewed as a nation of peace.

America will rightfully take its place in the world community as a cooperative partner and a genuine beacon of hope.

And here at home, America will finally be using its vast wealth and resources to promote the general welfare for all its citizens, not just the privileged few.

The birthright of every citizen born in our great nation, one which encourages all of its citizens to reach their full potential, one which assures each of its citizens a fair share of its vast wealth, one which encourages its citizens to participate in the greatest experiment in self-government in history, will be honored and revered, and the vision of our Founding Fathers renewed and reinstated to its rightful place.

Peace and prosperity are there for the taking.

All we have to do is truly want it ... and work for it.

Let's start by demanding our *Peace Dividend*.

We'll let our politicos know that we've got their number.

We'll put them on notice that the silly games are over.

We'll make them end all the unnecessary wars and chest-thumping.

We'll begin rebuilding our country and our hopes for the future.

We'll get things under control ... *our* control!

We'll each put our $14,952 Peace Dividend refund to work for us.

We'll go from there and see where it takes us.

Wherever that is surely will be better than where we've been.

Related Books by John Rachel

"An Unlikely Truth"

In this political drama, a bright, young, idealistic, Green Party candidate in his bid for the congressional seat of a conservative district in Ohio, teams with a beautiful, fiery African-American intern to combat the slick deceptions and ruthless tactics of a sweet-talking right wing incumbent.

Amazon (Kindle): amzn.to/1jetpiY
Amazon (Print): amzn.to/1lddvsp
Barnes & Noble: bit.ly/1l5FmuG
Apple iBook: bit.ly/1gT2O7w
Smashwords: bit.ly/1fIU3Mq

"Candidate Contracts: Taking Back Our Democracy"

Prepare to understand contemporary politics as never before! Prepare to see the future of American democracy! This manifesto offers a detailed, step-by-step plan for cleaning up the corruption in Washington DC. This is electoral reform so radical that in one master stroke, it puts America on the path to a healthy economy and directly addresses its #1 and #2 challenges: the suicidal march to war and the destructive impact of a historically high level of wealth inequality.

Amazon (Kindle): amzn.to/1QJRiNZ
Amazon (Print): amzn.to/1Cuq0du
Barnes & Noble: bit.ly/1GpTTLq
Apple iBook: apple.co/1BXnPcy
Smashwords: bit.ly/1B4DQCp
Kobo: bit.ly/1QETE64

"Fighting for the Democracy We Deserve"

This is a manual for constructive voting in the 2016 election. It presents a concrete plan for wresting control of the country and our democracy back from the rich and powerful, and restoring the constitutional mandate of government of the people, by the people, and for the people. It's not just more whining.
It's a real plan!

Amazon (Kindle): amzn.to/1VMf2Ft
Amazon (Print): amzn.to/1L9SdIC
Direct from printer: bit.ly/1i7ISFM
Amazon CA: amzn.to/1in513n
Amazon GB: amzn.to/1KfjtQO
Amazon JP: amzn.to/1OMslBG

About the Author

John Rachel has a B.A. in Philosophy, is a novelist and established political blogger. He has written eight novels. His political pieces have appeared at OpEdNews, Russia Insider, Greanville Post, and other alternative media outlets.

Since leaving the U.S. in 2006, he has lived in and explored 32 countries. He is now somewhat rooted in a traditional, rural Japanese community about an hour from Osaka, where he lives with his wife of four years. Daily he rides his bicycle through the soybean fields and rice paddies which sprawl across the surrounding landscape. As of the date of the release of this book, he has a small but promising organic vegetable garden which begs his attention.

You can follow his writing and the evolution of his world view at:

http://jdrachel.com

Legal Notices and Disclaimers

The Peace Dividend: The Most Controversial Proposal in the History of the World is an original work protected under international copyright law and registered with the U. S. Library of Congress © John D Rachel 2016.

It is an expansion and updating of ideas offered in *Candidate Contracts: Taking Back Our Democracy, Fighting for the Democracy We Deserve*, both published in 2015, and several blogs and political articles appearing in progressive media outlets, which appeared over the past four years.